Praise for *The Girly Thoughts 10-Day Detox Plan*

"True beauty comes from inside, not from how you look, but how you feel about how you look. We can be our own worst enemies, but now we have our own Wonder Woman in Dr. O'Gorman, who has empowered us by not only giving our self-doubt a label—girly thoughts—but also by giving us tools to detox from our negative self-beliefs. Every woman who ever wondered if she was "good enough" needs to read this book."

—**Karina Brez,** Miss Florida USA 2012

"Girly thoughts embody our unhealthy habit of cutting ourselves off at the knees by listening to the fearful little girl inside all of us who occasionally swims to the surface and sabotages the confident woman that we have worked so hard to become. Patricia O'Gorman has a bold and effective cease-and-desist plan that helps us silence all that inner trash talk, getting us instead to always speak from a place of strength, not weakness. She does it with charm, insight, and a beautifully written, simple, and effective program."

—**Monica Parker**, bestselling author of *Getting Waisted: A Survival Guide to Being Fat in a Society That Loves Thin*

"As women, we must learn to love ourselves before we can hope to be loved by others. Labeling our toxic inner dialogue as 'girly thoughts' is the first step in that journey. Sex, weight, body image, marriage, aging, parenting—they're all parts of each of us, yet we let our girly thoughts tell us we aren't good enough at any of them. Dr. O'Gorman's detox plan will shove those negative thoughts to the curb; every woman who reads this book will be empowered to continue her journey to become the strong and resilient goddess she is inside!"

—**Pamela Madsen,** author of *Shameless: How I Ditched the Diet, Got Naked, Found True Pleasure . . . and Somehow Got Home in Time to Cook Dinner*

"Patricia O'Gorman, Ph.D., has once again exhibited her winning combination of clinical expertise and her gift to inspire and engage her readers. In *The Girly Thoughts 10-Day Detox Plan,* she delivers a highly readable, practical guide to quieting those self-defeating messages of 'shoulds,' 'oughts,' and 'not-good-enoughs' that so often plague the female gender. This guide belongs on the nightstand of every woman who's ever-put herself down and/or put her own needs last."

—**Mary Eileen Williams,** author of
Feisty Side of Fifty and blogger for the Huffington Post

"Liberation is the promise of Dr. Patricia O'Gorman's newest book. And she delivers. All of Dr. O'Gorman's previous work has led her to this profound understanding of how women imprison themselves in what she calls "inner trash talk." Taking the cultural message down to the deeply personal, she leads us from the identification to the healing. Not content to reveal the problem, O'Gorman takes us by the hand and walks us into liberation.

—**Julie Bowden, M.S.,** psychotherapist and coauthor of
Recovery: A Guide for Adult Children of Alcoholics

"True beauty is expressed through inner strength and conviction. Patricia O'Gorman has revealed hers by courageously writing this brilliant book that will help you find yours through showing you simply and clearly how to get rid of your toxic, self-limiting beliefs and be true to you. As the father of two wonderful, strong women and as a therapist-psychiatrist committed to helping women find their voices, I applaud Dr. O'Gorman's important message!"

—**Bick Wanck, M.D.,** founder-owner of Bick Wanck M.D. & Associates,
founder-member of the American Academy of Addiction Psychiatry, and
author of *Mind Easing: Three Layers of Healing for Your Mind*

"Dr. O'Gorman offers some 'Aha!' moments to those who may not recognize their own self-sabotage, and offers suggestions and encouragement to change those counterproductive behaviors."

—**Michaela K. Rodeno,** CEO (retired), corporate director,
vintner, and author of *From Bubbles to Boardrooms*

"Through her skillful writing, Dr. O'Gorman describes a simple and clear way to identify and address toxic self-talk, and as always she uses terrific examples and practical information. I love this book."

—**Kathryn Brohl, LMFT,** author of *Social Service Workplace Bullying: A Betrayal of Good Intentions*

The **Girly** Thoughts
10-Day Detox Plan

The Resilient Woman's Guide to Saying NO
to Negative Self-Talk and YES to Personal Power

Patricia A. O'Gorman, Ph.D.

Health Communications, Inc.
Deerfield Beach, Florida

www.hcibooks.com

Library of Congress Cataloging-in-Publication Data

O'Gorman, Patricia A.

The girly thoughts 10-day detox plan : the resilient woman's guide to saying no to negative self-talk and yes to personal power / Patricia O'Gorman, PhD.

   p. cm

Includes bibliographical references.

1. Self-esteem in women. 2. Women—Psychology. 3. Self-talk. 4. Negativism.
5. Resilience (Personality trait) I. Title.
BF697.5.S46O46 2014
155.3'3391--dc23

                2014031148

ISBN-13: 978-0-7573-1815-3 (paperback)
ISBN-10: 0-7573-1815-0 (paperback)
ISBN-13: 978-0-7573-1816-0 (ePub)
ISBN-10: 0-7573-1816-9 (ePub)

Publisher: Health Communications, Inc.
          3201 S.W. 15th Street
          Deerfield Beach, FL 33442–8190

Cover design by Dane Wesolko
Interior design and formatting by Lawna Patterson Oldfield

To my sister Kathy.

It's hard to fight an enemy who has outposts in your head.

—Sally Kempton

Contents

Acknowledgments

Candace, thank you doesn't capture it . . . but thanks all the same. I couldn't have done this without you. You are the world's *best* developmental editor. With each book—and we're now up to three—I more deeply appreciate your wisdom, humor, and patience.

Christine, head of my team at HCI, thank you for believing in this book and supporting its birth—and me—through all of its birth pains. And to Peter and to my other team members at HCI, I offer my gratitude for your belief in my message.

I'd like to thank all the women in the talks I've given, my patients who shared their lives, and the media, as well as the subscribers to my blogs all who shared their enthusiasm for the concept of *girly thoughts* and demanded more. Your encouragement was largely responsible for this prequel to *The Resilient Woman*.

No effort of this magnitude devoted to help women *out* their most hidden, secret, self-destructive thoughts could be accomplished alone. My gratitude goes to my friends, particularly to Elie, Marie, Cynthia, Teena, Ellen, Elaine, Barbara, and Marsha, who patiently kept saying, "Are you done yet?" To my husband, Rob, who was in incredible good cheer as he fed me, emptied the dishwasher, and kept asking, "What can I do?" and made me laugh and laugh. And since he knows me so well, he was a great sounding board for my own *girly thoughts* about being able to finish this work as completely as I wanted it to be and on time. To my sons, Jeremy and Michael, and their girlfriends, Katie and Kaci, who are just so incredibly generous, creative, supportive, kind, loving, and patient.

As women we are in part created by those women who influence us, our own personal tribe or posse. These are the women who go largely unrecognized, except by us. I'd like to acknowledge mine— my mother and her sisters, all feisty, incredibly funny, bright women who fought back against the unfairness they encountered with the tools they had, teaching me not to accept what was offered just because it was, well, offered; my grandmother, whose struggles were never as apparent as her strengths; my family of strong and loving women in PEI who taught me so much, including how to bake; and my beautiful sister, who always believed in me. Frankie, who is sharing that life can go strong at ninety. Ruth Sondheimer, who helped me understand and love myself; Sophie Elam, who did for me what she did for scores of others at CCNY: forced me to see our potential and use it, making me one of "Sophie's Girls." Marty Mann, who early in my career told me "Don't let those boys get away with this," and thus beginning my learning in how to make it in what was then a "Man's World"; Joanne Dobson, who encouraged me to write, really write.

And thanks to my summer intern, Jen, for all of your incredible energy and creativity; and thanks to the sweet little one in my life, my Tribal, who knows how to calm me down with a lick and a snuggle.

Introduction

The truth will set you free.
But first it will piss you off.

—Gloria Steinem

Abandon anything about your life and habits that
might be holding you back: fortune favors action.

—Sophie Amoruso

I once heard a comedian open his act with this story:

> So, my girlfriend and I are cuddled up on the coach and I ask her, "What are you afraid of?"
>
> She gets all teary and says, "That you'll meet someone else. That you'll leave me, and I'll be all alone. What are you afraid of?" she asks, all choked up.
>
> "Snakes," I say, shrugging.

"No," I heard myself saying to his girlfriend as he was speaking. "You should be afraid of your *girly thoughts!*"

Girly thoughts? I've developed that term to give you a name for the toxic inner voice that robs you of your personal power by

1

focusing you instead on counterproductive messages, including:

- I am too smart or too assertive to be desirable.
- I am too fat, skinny, or busty to be attractive.
- It's my fault my husband had an affair.

Girly thoughts are your inner, negative self-talk that tell you how you should and should not be as a woman, what you can anticipate when you are a "good girl," and the price you can expect to pay when you step outside the often subtle societal standards you have been conditioned to follow.

Your girly thoughts are your own internalized criteria for how you should think, act, and most important, look. They are pretty exacting, too. When you step outside those values, you can expect to pay a price through some type of rejection, particularly from those you are close to—and even from yourself.

Your girly thoughts are the part of you that pushes too hard to be accepted and acceptable and that acts like your own inner Mean Girls club—the part of you that has internalized society's messages. And because you are forcing yourself to fit into a mold, you often feel like a fraud, as though you'll be found out and rejected because you are not really acting in accordance with what is best for you or with whom you really are. You have been influenced by many cultural factors and social norms during the twenty or thirty or sixty-plus years you've been on this planet, and these factors and norms have shaped your reasoning, your reactions and responses, and even your feelings. So when you have such a thought, you are sometimes tempted to embrace it as reality, particularly when it is backed up by intense feelings—you feel sad, or frightened, or just not good enough—and you take that as further evidence that your thought is correct.

Your girly thoughts are so believable to you because you have been conditioned to think this way. As a result, your girly thoughts represent a very powerful part of how you organize your identity. But they do not tell the full story. Unfortunately, you may sometimes believe that they do, since they generate almost overwhelming feelings that make you feel compelled to take an action or make a decision without thinking it through. So you confront a colleague, spend too much on clothes, or end a relationship and then collapse in despair.

Girly thoughts is a term that was coined by a colleague of mine, psychologist Tom Lund, when we were speaking about *this thing* women do to themselves. "Girly thoughts," he said, and my jaw dropped. It perfectly captured the unique way we women treat—or should I say, mistreat—ourselves. I love the term because it has a certain energy to it; it gains your attention and repels you just a little, doesn't it? It's grating, dismissive, and a little demeaning— which is just what girly thoughts do to you!

The Price We Pay

Our society has a very narrow cultural norm for what a desirable woman is: young, attractive, thin, sexy, not too smart, and certainly not too aggressive. Most of us spend our adult lives chasing this impossible ideal—but in reality even fashion models don't look like their cover photos, in real life! And let's face it: when you do reach a magic goal, like getting the promotion you worked hard for, you still never feel good enough about the other things.

Remember when you were very thin but still believed you were not thin *enough*? Think back to when you felt most beautiful but worried that your date would find another woman more attractive. Have you ever had just the right combination of physical appeal and brain power to gather the attention you really want? This self-doubt, lack of confidence, or sense of never being good enough is the price we pay when we let girly thoughts take up residence in our minds.

Good Girls

Your girly thoughts are also the result of how you have internalized the message to be a good girl, how you made sense of the world as a young girl. They represent your beliefs, your dreams, and what it means to be a woman. You were fertile soil as you were growing up, and messages of what women are and what kind of woman you wanted to be took root. You were impressionable. You believed a great deal of what you were told and what you saw. The world you lived in helped you form certain opinions about yourself and shaped your dreams of what you wanted to be, what kind of adult you saw yourself becoming.

Your burgeoning girly thoughts were unconscious, and they've remained that way for the most part—until now. Your girly thoughts formed over time and through numerous sources of input, and they are reinforced every day through your family of origin, intimate relationships, friendships, business and professional influences, family pressures, and, most especially, media.

Your girly thoughts are what you were taught to believe in and who you were told to be. Like an old friend, your girly thoughts also helped you understand your experiences, providing an important frame of reference not only for your expectations of what the world had to offer you, but also for whom you should value, whom you should find attractive, whom you should see as a threat, and what you should look for in others.

Girly Thoughts Lead to Toxic Self-Talk

Your girly thoughts provide a handy script for toxic self-talk. Think about the last time you looked at yourself in the mirror: did you love everything you saw there? If you're like most women, the answer is a resounding *no*. But what really matters is what you told yourself as you looked at your reflection. If that was some version of "I need to lose a few more pounds," or "I wish I could afford a boob job so I would look sexier," or "I look so old; I'll never get that job. Maybe I should color my hair so I look younger for the job interview," that was your girly thoughts talking and feeding you a steady stream of toxic self-talk instead of helping you address your real concern.

Girly Thoughts Can Lead to Feeling Like an Impostor

Even when you appear fine on the outside—you have a great career, a loving family, a devoted partner, and a healthy lifestyle— do you feel vulnerable on the inside, where you live with and speak to yourself? Do you feel like a fraud, just waiting to be found out? Or that whatever you have on the outside feels transitory, as if it could be taken away because on some level you feel not deserving enough? When you do achieve a goal, does part of you believe that it happened by accident or by luck rather than by your own hard work and determination?

Girly Thoughts Can Lead to Depression, Codependency, and Even Addiction

You're filled with doubt, and you're even filled with anger directed from you to you, and so you silence yourself. This is how your girly thoughts can result in depression and anxiety, the source of which may feel unclear; this makes you feel just a little nuts, because, after all, you *are* productive, so why do you feel so bad? You ask yourself, *What's wrong with me?* and your girly thoughts provide a ready answer that results in you doubting your attractiveness, your effectiveness, and your desirability as you second-guess yourself at every turn, never giving yourself a break and never coming up for air.

You may numb yourself by throwing yourself into trying to help others with their problems, but this is a form of codependency that tells you to be the good girl by being so available as a way to distract you from what is going on inside you. Or you may try to anesthetize, or "reward," yourself with food, wine, shopping, gambling, or excessive exercise, all to focus and calm yourself and perhaps have some release.

So you speak to yourself in your own mind in a harsh way to motivate yourself, and you use a tone that you would not use with someone you love: your partner, your child, or any other family member. You may berate yourself, calling yourself stupid, or worse; you push yourself to lose weight, get your hair under control, and not be so sensitive to office politics.

When you berate yourself, your girly thoughts are distracting and disempowering you by focusing your attention on the wrong things. Girly thoughts have you concentrate on something other than your goal, and they make it more complicated to achieve what you had planned and to feel good about your ability to accomplish what is important to you. Girly thoughts consume your energy, diminish your self-esteem, and cause you to not value yourself or take care of yourself.

All women have girly thoughts. Even when you come from a supportive background, have a compassionate family, and don't let the opinions of others color your opinion of yourself, you are still subject to those media-fed adolescent feelings of insecurity racing through your head for the rest of your life. Even the most accomplished women often feel like they are faking it—that while they are seen by others as responsible and in charge, they feel out of control inside and fear that someone will find out.

Free Yourself to Live Your Life—Start Detoxing

When you are used to doing something, eating something, or thinking something that is not good for you, a detox plan can be helpful. This is why I've developed this ten-day program to help you detox from your girly thoughts.

In *The Girly Thoughts 10-Day Detox Plan*, you'll learn to identify the sources of those false standards, the things you are doing to yourself that sap your energy and are literally poisonous to your well-being. Together we will identify how your girly thoughts sabotage you in the major areas of your life. I will show you how to free yourself internally from the parts of being the good girl that do not work for you by teaching you to challenge your toxic self-talk.

This is, after all, an inside job. You'll learn to change those behaviors through a systematic program designed to move you away from your old belief system and embrace a new way based on who you really are. You'll replace the negative self-talk you've grown to believe is your truth. Through a day-by-day plan, you will begin to change your thinking, see new possibilities, and enjoy your life by freeing up your creative energy and stepping into your personal power.

You will learn to develop new skills to replace this unproductive way of defining who you are. You will begin to like, appreciate, and, most importantly, value your abilities, your quirks, and even your looks as you learn to embrace your inner resources to uncover the powerful woman you truly are.

I first introduced the term *girly thoughts* in my book, *The Resilient Woman: Mastering the 7 Steps to Personal Power*, and I have expanded the concept here. As I've written and spoken to women about it, the reception has been tremendous both in the United States and internationally. In many ways, *The Girly Thoughts 10-Day Detox Plan* is a prequel to that book. I discovered that many women continued to struggle with mastering their sense of personal power because they lacked a clear and doable strategy for eliminating their toxic girly thoughts. This book is that strategy.

Once you understand where your negative self-talk originated, how it continues to be nurtured by many internal and external influences, and how you are hurting yourself by allowing—even perhaps encouraging—those toxic messages to reside and flourish in your mind, you'll be on your way to eliminating them and creating a new internal voice that empowers and protects you.

Now let's start detoxing from those girly thoughts.

Girly Thoughts

Thanks to the many women I have spoken to, treated, and met through their articles on blogs and in magazines, through books, and through movies, I have developed a list of actual girly thoughts. These are the ones I have found to be the most common, the ones we trip over the most.

This is what you are thinking:

Girly thought #1:
I'm fat.

Girly thought #2:
I hate my body because I don't look like a model or a movie star.

Girly thought #3:
I'm a good girl, and good girls don't . . .

Girly thought #4:
I must keep my partner sexually happy, or else . . .

Girly thought #5:
Someone loving me will fill the hole in me.

Girly thought #6:

Being married proves I'm lovable.

Girly thought #7:

I'm getting old, and I have to do something.

Girly thought #8:

I'll seem younger and sexier if I sound like a little girl.

Girly thought #9:

I can't get as far as a guy at work.

Girly thought #10:

I can't do that—what if I fail?

Girly thought #11:

I need to be seen as nice at work.

Girly thought #12:

The women I work with are my biggest competition— or my best friends.

Girly thought #13:

I'm not financially secure without a man.

Girly thought #14:

I'm no good with numbers.

Girly thought #15:

It's okay for my daughter to play at being sexy.

Girly thought #16:

I feel I should be my daughter's best friend, but I don't have any influence over her.

PART I

YOUR NEGATIVE SELF-TALK: What It Is and Where It Came From

*In an effort to be mature and independent . . .
a woman tries to be more and more perfect because
the only way she can alleviate her dependence
on that judgmental voice is to be
perfect enough to shut it up.*

—Marion Woodman

*You hardly ever see a smart
woman with a dumb guy.*

—Erica Jong

In the first three days of this program, you will get to know yourself and how your girly thoughts function throughout your life, insinuating themselves into your self-worth, telling you that you are either perfect or nothing. You will learn about your inner strengths and the particular role your family had in teaching and reinforcing your girly thoughts.

Keep a Journal on Your Progress

I encourage you to begin a journal that will serve as your personal *Girly Thoughts Detox Workbook*. Not only will it serve to keep all your thoughts and notes together (if you're like me, you probably already have enough grocery lists and scraps of messages to yourself at the bottom of your purse), but more important, it will provide a personal and concrete plan for moving into your personal power, your resilience.

Your journal can be bound; you can keep it on your tablet, laptop, e-reader, or even on your smartphone; or you can even create a Pinterest board. Make it something easy to use and available.

Your journal will function in several ways:

- As a benchmark—much like your initial weigh-in when you begin a diet
- To note your answers to the exercises
- As a record of how you have been able to change your thinking
  - ➤ An account of what has worked for you personally
  - ➤ All the random "aha!" moments that will occur as you wrap your mind around how your girly thoughts are both a daily confidence drain and an energy waster in your life

➤ The solutions you are developing for countering this

➤ A source of strength that convinces you that you can do it

- As a reminder, after you have completed your girly thoughts detox program and revisited your answers to the initial exercises, of how much you have changed

No, *You're Not Crazy*: Those Are Just Your Girly Thoughts

You could have all the crazy thoughts you wanted, as long as you smiled and kept them to yourself.

—Mara Purnhagen

Men are taught to apologize for their weaknesses, women for their strengths.

—Lois Wyse

As women, we all think girly thoughts. We smile even when we are uncomfortable. We don't talk about what we really fear or about how inadequate we feel. We don't share the toxic inner messages that make us doubt ourselves; we're afraid that we are the only ones who feel this way and that if we do say anything, everyone will know we're nuts. The result is that we *do* feel crazy. But we're not! We are just having girly thoughts. A well-dressed woman took me aside after a recent talk I delivered to executive women and said, "I always thought it was me, that perhaps I was just a little nuts. I'm so relieved to now know it's really all of us."

Girly Thoughts: A Learned Way of Th

Your girly thoughts provide a vital service by helping you make sense of what is happening around and within you. They developed as a way for you to understand cause and effect in your world. Unfortunately, they are also a result of how you've learned to blame yourself for anything that is hurtful to you, which becomes a toxic form of self-talk that comes out like this:

- I'm so stupid; I should have known he'd do this.
- Who do I think I am that I could pull this off?
- When will I learn that I'm too smart and I'd better stop showing it?

It's not that we shouldn't look at our part in things that don't go well or don't go according to plan—of course we should. It's actually very useful to do so, because that will help us develop insight. But merely understanding your role in something is not the same as taking complete responsibility for things that are not fully your doing.

For many women, girly thoughts act like a conduit through which all their discomfort and all the stresses of their life are filtered. You are probably one of these women. When something goes wrong, do you do any of the following?

- Check to see how you might have caused it.
- Blame the poor actions of others on:
  - ➤ Something you did or didn't do
  - ➤ Something you said
  - ➤ How you made them feel
  - ➤ How you looked

And when something goes right, do you do either of the following?

- Credit the circumstance instead of yourself.
- Give credit to others and take little to none for yourself.

Girly Thoughts Become Toxic Self-Talk

Over time, this way of looking through a lens of negative thinking begins to make even more sense. Your girly thoughts explain why you are regarded the way you are. They help you anticipate how you will be treated. In this way, your girly thoughts become a toxic belief system that keeps you stuck.

Once you get used to thinking this way, you'll continue to do so, because this is how you have learned to make sense of the world. But your girly thoughts are poisonous to your self-esteem. They drain you of your energy, sap your creativity, reduce your confidence, and diminish your productivity by keeping you all tied up in knots about things that, in the greater scheme of things, are not that important: So what if you've gained five pounds? Why does it matter that you came on strong with a coworker? Why do you attribute your success to luck instead of your own hard work? Do you always have to be a good girl? Your world won't end, even if it *feels* like it will.

There are a number of toxic beliefs and feelings created by girly thoughts.

Self-Doubt

On a basic level, your girly thoughts make you feel insecure about your hair, height, weight, age, and just about anything else.

Your girly thoughts function as an internal gauge of perfection against which you measure yourself, and guess what? You find yourself falling short of what you think you should be.

As a result of your girly thoughts, you begin to really doubt yourself. Gone is the enthusiasm you had as a young girl. Remember when you believed you could be president? That you could marry a great guy? That you were smart, charming, and funny? These empowering thoughts became replaced by concern about what others are thinking of you, even by a fear that they are judging you, because at times you feel like a fraud. Your girly thoughts force you to act in a way that is not in line with who you are. You may feel vulnerable and judged by the following:

- Friends
- Coworkers
- Other mothers
- Wives and girlfriends of work associates
- Daughters
- In-laws
- Boyfriends or husbands
- Your family

Jealousy

Do you recall feeling threatened by a look your boyfriend or husband gave another woman? Your girly thoughts pit woman against woman by having you constantly measuring yourself against others to see who is prettier, who is thinner, who has bigger breasts, who is better dressed, or who reveals too much cleavage.

And when you don't quite measure up, your girly thoughts are there to provide a running commentary of your flaws.

Self-Silencing

Instead of supporting you, your girly thoughts cause you to run the other way. Have you ever wished you could just vanish because you have a run in your pantyhose, you got a bad haircut, or you forgot to put on mascara before you left the house? Many women spend a fair amount of time wishing they were invisible because of some physical imperfection of which they are acutely aware but that no one else probably even notices. When this happens to you, do you tend to silence yourself, hoping that no one will notice you?

Taking Responsibility

It almost doesn't matter what the problem is: if there *is* a problem, you scan yourself to see whether you are somehow to blame. Frequently, you come up with something you have done that *might* have contributed to the problem, so you assume responsibility as you have been programmed to do.

Have you ever had these or similar thoughts?

- You cheated on me because I'm fat.
- I'm too old to be sexy.
- Even though my coworker was sick, I should have finished that report on time by myself, so he wouldn't get in trouble.

These are the types of thoughts we have when we internalize responsibility for others. As women, we have been programmed to look within ourselves and find the cause for the hurtful, unfair behavior of others; we blame ourselves and let *them* off the hook for injuring us. Our girly thoughts have us so focused on our looks and our actions that we see these parts of who we are as culpable for the poor actions of others. And if we even get up the nerve to confront those who hurt us, we often filter our wounded feelings through our girly thoughts.

This is not only inaccurate, it is also confusing, and over time this taking of responsibility that isn't yours also begins to condition others that *you* are more answerable for the ways they've hurt you than *they* are. The vicious cycle begins: you feel harmed; you become very emotional and blame yourself. The other person backs away from responsibility by citing that you are just too emotional, and—bingo!—*you* have become the problem. If repeated enough, this cycle could result in your developing codependency, a type of learned helplessness in which you believe that your only possible choice is to take care of someone else because you can't determine how to care for yourself (Oliver-Diaz and O'Gorman, 1988).

Lack of Confidence

Your girly thoughts drain your confidence by telling you that you can't accomplish what it is you set out to do. They cause you to not take any action, or they undermine the actions you do take, stymie your creativity, and thwart your positive risk taking by providing you with an ongoing list of everything that is wrong with you. In this way, any confidence you have that is based on what you have achieved in your life—from your education to your productivity at work to the relationships you cherish—is drained away, and this makes you feel inadequate, less-than, and inferior.

Your girly thoughts accomplish this by constantly telling you the following:

- You're too aggressive.
- You'd better not speak until you have *all* the facts.
- You can't go out looking like *that*.
- People will see through you.
- No one will take you seriously, and you'll feel ashamed.

Fear of Risk Taking

Taking risks is an important part of life. Much of your success in life is a result of your own efforts, what you have made happen. Whether this involved pushing to go to the college where you felt the most comfortable or applying for a job even though you didn't quite have everything the employers said they wanted, you risked listening to and trusting yourself.

Think back to a time you didn't take an action because you feared any of the following:

- You would be laughed at.
- People would ask, "Who do you think you are?"
- You'd never recover if it didn't go well.
- People would call you a bitch.

The Good Girl

You've probably realized by now that playing by the rules does not ensure that your life will go smoothly. Being rewarded for being the good girl is a myth that goes along with needing to be rescued by Prince Charming. Rules are important, but they should not dictate how you act, how you feel, and or how you judge yourself.

Focusing on being the good girl is a surefire way to set yourself up for a fall. Life is full of challenges for everyone, whether or not the rules are strictly followed. Being a good girl does not insulate you from having bad things happen to you. I wish I could count how many times women have tearfully told me the following:

- But I've done everything I was supposed to do, even though it's been hard.
- I've sacrificed.
- I've followed the rules.
- I've done all the right things, so why is this happening to me?

Their codependency was alive and well. They were taking care of others, not themselves, and were living the definition of the good girl.

Girly Thoughts Sap Your Personal Power

Your girly thoughts have you second-guessing yourself, and putting your vital but finite energy into places that drain you and don't get you any closer to your goal. In this way, your girly thoughts sap your power by directing your attention and focus away from what is important to you and instead tie you up in knots about some *inner fault*. Here's how it works:

- You don't speak up in client meetings because you fear you'll be judged.
- You caution yourself not to be too brainy as you get ready for a date.
- You post a ten-year-old photo on the dating website you join because no one will find you attractive the way you are.

How to Know You're Having Girly Thoughts

When you have a term for something, you naturally feel more control over it. You can wrap your mind around it, analyze it, and capture it in a new way. Coastal tribes of the northern regions of the world, who are often collectively called by the umbrella term "Eskimos," are said to have dozens, even hundreds, of words for snow, because each word describes a different condition that is important to plan for, recognize, and master.

Similarly, when you have a term (like *girly thoughts*) for something as important as the negative inner dialogue so common to women, you have a way of encapsulating this experience, looking at it, and determining what is really going on; thus freeing you to find ways to maneuver around it. It becomes something you can engage with, rather than it just being a part of who you are that you are powerless to do anything about.

You might be thinking, *I'm good. I've gotten this far without addressing girly thoughts, so why do I need to do this now?* If this is what you're thinking, please answer the following questions:

- Are you critical of your body shape or size? (insecurity)
- Are you critical of your age? (insecurity)
- Do you begin a statement or questions with "I'm sorry, but . . ."? (insecurity)
- Do you live in fear of your partner leaving you for someone more attractive, younger, smarter, or less of a threat? (jealousy)
- Do you secretly feel good when another woman fails at something? (jealousy)
- Do you second-guess yourself about what you wear, how you look, or what you just said, hoping no one will notice? (self-silencing)

- Have you ever not shared something in a meeting be
  you were afraid someone might disagree or even cha
  (self-silencing)
- When you encounter misfortune, do you blame yourself by
  thinking or saying, *I'm not* . . . [fill in the blank], *so I deserve
  this?* (taking responsibility)
- Do you believe that the problems or misfortunes of others are
  somehow your responsibility to fix? (taking responsibility)
- Do you worry that you are *too* smart, aggressive, tall, heavy,
  or old? (lack of confidence)
- Do you fear that you'll never have your dreams come true
  because you don't have the education, connections, or luck
  you'll need? (lack of confidence)
- Do you ever refuse to take action because you fear you
  could fail? (fear of risk taking)
- Do you pass up opportunities to try new or different things because
  you fear people will think you are crazy? (fear of risk taking)
- Do you think you have to do everything right or else you are
  totally wrong? (good girl)
- Do you feel pulled in a million directions, trying to please
  everyone? (good girl)
- Do you think you have to *earn* love? (good girl)

If you answer yes to even one of these questions, your girly
thoughts are alive and well. Now ask yourself, *Is this how I want to
continue to live my life?*

The Life Cycle of Girly Thoughts

Your girly thoughts are cultivated throughout your life by what
may seem to be random events. But each of these events affected

you, and what were initially random events, like being called bossy in day care, inform your beliefs about yourself and the world.

Your identity is formed in part by your girly thoughts. They profoundly influence how you come to see the world and understand your role in it, and they are reinforced on so many levels—from your family to the media to what you read in school to how your friends act.

It All Begins So Innocently

Recently, a man who interviewed me told me that the teachers at his two-year-old granddaughter's daycare center had said she was bossy. He asked, "How bad can that be?"

My response was that if the only time this little girl was called bossy was when she took charge, assumed leadership, or solved a problem, it most likely would not be a problem—as long as the label was used only once or twice.

But if we look at this throughout a typical girl's lifetime and add other important statements made by those in authority about who she is, we'll see results like those you may have personally experienced.

Being called bossy as a toddler sends a message to the girl that she is doing something wrong, even though if you ask her about her behavior, you'll hear her delight in figuring things out, relishing her power to make things happen and to be helpful.

In grade school, she may always have her hand up, and she'll learn that this is somehow unbecoming when she is called a know-it-all. At home she may be reminded to be the good girl, which often means being the quiet, compliant girl. In her tweens, she quits her soccer team and becomes a fashionista who is more focused on her looks and on what she wears than on how to learn to avoid personalizing defeat. By the time she reaches puberty, she has learned that it is more important to be liked than to be smart, and she starts dumbing down (Martin, 2007).

In her quest for acceptance, she may develop a subtle eating disorder as she attempts to stay thin. Her natural desire to explore her world and attempt new things is squelched by the disapproval of those whose opinions are deemed important. She becomes anxious, depressed, and uncertain, and doesn't know why. Her family may notice and think she needs medication. But whatever her mental health diagnosis might be, an underlying factor is her girly thoughts, which are fully developed and are now running her life.

And it all began with being called bossy in day care.

Sugar and Spice and Everything Nice

Remember the nursery rhyme "What Are Little Girls Made Of?" In a similar way, your girly thoughts are composed of several key elements that all serve to reinforce one another:

- Early messages you received about your looks, behavior, and dress
- Constant reminders to be the good girl
- Media images of who you should be and how you should look
- Female traditions in your family that reinforced being pleasing to others and making others comfortable as a first priority, even if that means putting your needs second

And then there's stress. Our girly thoughts become the funnel through which we also experience and understand stressors. We come to see the cause of whatever happens to us and others through our girly thoughts, and they become our default ratio-nalization for why we feel slighted, or worse. As a result of this reasoning, we learn to blame ourselves for so many things that we are not responsible for, situations that we are as caught in as everyone else, and we learn to attribute our successes to someone else's doing instead of crediting ourselves and our positive—even outstanding—accomplishments.

Where Do You Find Girly Thoughts?

Every aspect of life is affected by your girly thoughts:

- Your relationships as a daughter, a granddaughter, a niece, an aunt, and a cousin
- Your view of your physical self, especially as you age
- The search for someone special: dating, falling in love, getting married, and even staying married
- Your relationships as a friend or a neighbor
- Your relationships in school, on the job, and in your community
- Your work
- Your dealings with money
- Your parenting

Girly thoughts influence you in all of your decision making as you attempt to do the following:

- Be the good girl in school
- Dress desirably as a preteen, look perfect as a teenager, and stay thin as a young adult
- Stay sexually desirable in middle age
- Continue to look young as you age

- Achieve success in your career
- Choose the right toys for your daughter

From Girly Thoughts to Personal Power

Your girly thoughts are your constant companion, forming a toxic inner dialogue that defines you in a less than favorable way. You deserve better!

So it's time to make a decision. Do you want to change your thinking? If so, welcome to this exploration of you that you've just named, a part of you so ingrained that it hasn't even been conscious until now. You are about to undertake the most amazing journey that will change your life.

When you filter the world through your girly thoughts, unfortunate events become understood in the context of your age or looks or other personal attributes, even if the situation has nothing to do with those—even if what happens is all about the other person and not you. But the good news is that you can unlearn your girly thoughts and learn to embrace your personal power, your resilience. Your resilience is made conscious by acknowledging the skills you developed from going through the tough times in your life, and it is having those strengths form part of your identity. As a result, it is about walking in your own personal power—the direct opposite of your girly thoughts (O'Gorman, 2013).

Learned Behavior

Your brain can assist you in developing your personal power. New research shows that your brain is elastic, which means that it changes based on what you are exposed to and what sense you make of new experiences (Merzenich, 2013).

Learned behavior affects your brain, and so does the new information you use to make decisions. New stimulation and new schemata cause your brain to slightly reorganize so it can use these new facts. You can move out of old ways of thinking to make room for new ways of understanding by identifying what is not working and then reprogramming this part of your brain (actually changing your wiring by introducing new ways of understanding yourself in the world). Saying no to toxic self-talk and embracing your personal power is one example of doing this.

Now it's time to take charge and retrain those brain cells by doing the following:

- **Identifying** your girly thoughts, especially those of which you haven't even been aware
- **Weaning** yourself from this type of unproductive thinking through a series of gradual steps
- **Replacing** this thinking with accurate thoughts about yourself by building new ways of reasoning that embrace your strengths and personal power
- **Redefining** who you are, once you push aside your girly thoughts, as you develop new behaviors and rewire your brain

As women, we are creative; we think big dreams. It's time to stop letting your toxic self-talk—your girly thoughts—define your boundaries. It's time to begin enjoying your life to its fullest.

Let's start by examining and reframing some of the ways you view yourself through exploring the Wonder Woman in you, the you full of possibilities and strengths.

DO'S & DON'TS

✓ Do stop berating yourself for having that ongoing, negative self-talk.

✓ Do have fun identifying your negative self-talk as girly thoughts.

✓ Do notice in what areas you are more likely to have girly thoughts.

✓ Do realize you don't need to continue your girly thoughts.

✗ Don't continue to allow your girly thoughts to sap your personal power.

✗ Don't let seemingly innocent (but actually toxic) comments about your daughter, young girls, or yourself pass without a response.

The Wonder Woman in You

*I'm just an ordinary Amazon, but I feel that
I can do things, so—I can do them!*

—Wonder Woman to a group of schoolgirls

*Although I grew up in very modest
and challenging circumstances, I consider
my life to be immeasurably rich.*

—Sonia Sotomayor

Wonder Woman, a superheroine cartoon originally created by an American psychologist and published by DC Comics in 1941, will finally come to the movie screen. Wonder Woman is a warrior princess who possesses a wide range of superhuman powers and an arsenal of personal weapons, including the Lasso of Truth, that give her superior combat and battle skills.

Being Wonder Woman doesn't sound too bad, does it? Let's face it; this is who we want to be—at least on days when we need a little extra something. Imagine being resilient and goal directed, shaking off the obstacles with your famous smile. Imagine flying around without being frustrated by needing to look for a parking spot. Imagine looking good in a bathing suit without needing to count calories. Imagine having magical powers and accomplishing good deeds for which you are recognized without needing to make the other guy look good. Imagine kicking the butts of the bad guys and still having your hair look great—and staying forever young. Who could say no to all that?

Superheroines in Your Life

Let me be honest about my admiration of Wonder Woman: I've been a fan of hers and of the few other heroines and superheroines celebrated in the media for some time. My veneration began with the largely forgotten TV series *Sheena, Queen of the Jungle* (which was a favorite of my mother's), based on the first female comic book character to have her own title. The bejeweled, platinum-haired Sheena spoke to animals (a skill I thought was very cool when I was a little girl), was reared in the jungle, and saved mostly men who wandered around her territory. I admired other cartoon characters, too, from Betty Boop, the first portrayal of a sexual woman in the 1930s, to the levelheaded Wilma Flintstone in the 1960s, to the recent addition of the cute and crafty Dora of *Dora the Explorer.*

Not all my heroines are of the cartoon variety, however, and, of course, neither are yours. We find many real-life heroines in the women in our personal lives: our mothers, a favorite sister, a grandmother, a friend, or a mentor. Some of my personal heroines are celebrated in the media: women like tennis champion Billie Jean King, First Lady Michelle Obama, TV anchor Robin Roberts, and actress Grace Park. Others should be famous but aren't yet: Navajo/Diné Dr. Cassandra Manuelito-Kerkvliet, the first

Native-American woman to be appointed president of a mainstream university; Dorothy Height, a women's rights and civil rights activist; Nellie Bly, an investigative journalist who exposed abuses at mental institutions; and Cecilia Payne, an early astronomer and astrophysicist who bowed to pressure to change her doctoral dissertation, which was later proved to have been correct.

But back to my cartoon heroine Wonder Woman.

Approximately forty male superheroes have been featured in major movie blockbusters since 2002, but now, with a female lead, the movie industry has to grapple with the fact that the comics have portrayed Wonder Woman not only as powerful but also as sexual (Dockterman, 2013). This is presenting a problem.

Hmm . . . sound familiar? Being seen as sexual when you don't want to be does take the fun out of being seen as powerful. In fact, in the battle of the sexes, this is often a way in which women feel minimized and diminished in power. As you know and have probably experienced firsthand, this is an either-or situation for women: you're either a brainless sexpot or an asexual, bossy bitch. At least that's the way it's been. (We'll look at this phenomenon more closely in Day 5 and Day 8.)

But times are changing. *The Hunger Games* (both the novels and the movie franchise) depict a powerful, sexy character, and the story—not the heroine's body—is the attraction. Now, isn't that how *you* want to be known? Your physical attributes are in there, but you're known by your story, your strengths, and even your resiliency, and the physical part of you is not seen as all you are.

At times, we women do a delicate dance in managing our strengths and resiliencies along with our vulnerabilities and our sexuality. But like Wonder Woman, you are coming into your season. It is time for you to embrace your strengths by learning to expose what gets in your way of being everything you can and should be: your girly thoughts.

Wonder Woman Beats Snow White

So many of us have been raised on fairy tales of the beautiful, vulnerable princess who needs to be rescued by a powerful, handsome man. This is an image that is deeply ingrained and becomes part of our girly thoughts, forming our image of how we should look: beautiful all the time, even when we are asleep because of an evil curse. It forms our image of how we should act: needy, tentative. And it programs us for what we should need: a powerful man to rescue us so we may live happily ever after.

So it's no surprise to me that Wonder Woman may finally be considered worthy of a movie. Why has it taken so long for her and other superheroines to come to the screen? Perhaps it's because these story lines do not revolve around the men in their lives. These are women on a mission.

Are women ready for this? The answer is yes. In the 1970s, actress Pam Grier (who is remembered mainly as Quentin Tarantino's titular character in *Jackie Brown*) appeared in films that made her "the biggest, baddest, and most beautiful of all female heroes in popular culture," according to Rikke Schubart, the author of *Super Bitches and Action Babes* (Cox, 2013). Yet with few exceptions, until very recently, sexual inequality ruled. Of the 157 female protagonists in action films released between 1991 and 2005 that Cox studied, only 7 percent took control of their situations; 58 percent were submissive to male characters. Thirty percent were

dead when the credits rolled. Is it any wonder that Snow White
has been the role model we've aspired to emulate?

What is the main difference between Wonder Woman and
Snow White? Snow White achieves her desires by being passive. In
fact, she is so delicate and vulnerable that she needs to be rescued
by dwarfs and a prince. Do we really find her appealing? Wonder
Woman has confidence in her abilities, and she takes action. No
rescuing needed here. In fact, she enjoys bringing justice to others.
Snow White can't hold a candle to Wonder Woman, and it isn't
even a close contest.

Your Self-Limiting Girly Thoughts

Think for a moment about just how much like Wonder Woman
you really are. You are resilient—you get knocked down and you
get up again—just like Wonder Woman. You are capable of doing
amazing things. You are beautiful in ways that surprise you. You
are able to rally your strengths and accomplish things that may
even astonish you.

But then an important difference becomes apparent. Wonder Woman knows she's resilient. She knows she can take care of
herself and the world. She believes in herself (no girly thoughts
here!). She knows there will be challenges; she expects rejection
but doesn't take it personally. In fact, she thrives on it—but do you?

You may have forgotten, or may never have fully accepted,
that you are indeed wonderful and powerful, that you have skills
and resources—perhaps untapped, but present nevertheless. Yet
instead of focusing on those strengths, skills, and resources, you've
learned to let your girly thoughts keep you focused on the wrong

things. When you are faced with challenges that range from losing the weight you gained while pregnant to finally handing in the report you keep editing, do you believe they are challenges only a superheroine can accomplish? When you struggle to end a relationship you know is really bad for you or find the right time to ask for a raise, do you give up inside before you even get started?

Perfection is the enemy of the good. It is a time and energy waster. Perfection is what your girly thoughts strive to achieve. But Wonder Woman is not concerned about being perfect; she merely wants to get the job done, and she does!

In fact, your girly thoughts may be so ingrained that you feel you should give up and not take care of yourself, that to do so makes you either selfish or bitchy. Fighting the label your girly thoughts warn you against can feel very risky even for an accomplished woman.

But your girly thoughts limit your power because they put you in a situation where you can't replenish yourself by paying attention to your own physical and emotional requirements. As a result, your very legitimate need to focus on your own needs goes underground. Those needs may then come out sideways: through caring intensely for others, which is called codependency, or anesthetizing through mind-numbing activities such as eating, shopping, gambling, or drinking, which (as we know) creates other problems. This is how it plays out. You may feel tired and stressed, have problems sleeping, or skip meals and then eat too much when you do get near food. You may really look forward to a beer or a glass of wine—perhaps a little too much—as a treat. You may stop exercising or justify your overindulgence at the casino because you think you deserve it. You dig yourself a hole.

What a Superheroine Like
You Really Deserves

You do indeed deserve many things. These include caring for yourself and being cared for by others. But most of all, what you really deserve is the knowledge to make yourself a worthy recipient of your own best efforts—your personal power.

Wonder Woman possesses knowledge of her personal power that allows her to take care of others, herself, and the world, yet she also has the resources to challenge herself as well as everyone else. Isn't this what you would like your personal power to do for you?

So what gets in the way of your self-care? On the surface, taking care of yourself seems like such a simple and obvious thing to do, doesn't it? You might answer that your inability to take care of yourself is the result of the needs of others you care about: your boyfriend, best friend, coworker, elderly father, children, husband, grandmother—the list goes on.

Or you might focus on the demands of others who ask you to do what they cannot (or will not) do for themselves: planning a party for a friend even if you don't have the time, taking your husband's shirts to the laundry when you're late for a meeting, bringing your boss coffee even though you have a report due in an hour, or refusing help even when you could use it.

Put on Your Own Mask First

You probably think that you can take care of yourself *once* you have completed what you believe you must first do for others. This reasoning puts you in second place in your life pretty routinely. I know you think you can wait, and let's face it: you've probably had a great deal of practice in waiting. For example, when you hear the preflight briefing that instructs "In case of a decompression, put on your own oxygen mask before assisting others," I would guess that most mothers probably think, *Oh, I can hold my breath and put on my child's mask first; I can wait.*

This is an expertise we have developed, so we might as well own it. We have learned that we can place ourselves second in many major categories in our lives, and we have learned not only to make this okay but to embrace it as altruistic. Rather stunning, isn't it?

Your Internal Heroine

I recently had lunch with a new friend, Marissa. We spoke, as new friends do, about our lives, our struggles, and what we have learned. Her life is fascinating in a way that falls under the category of "you can't make this stuff up."

Marissa's story involves a heroic journey of incredible intricacies, challenges, and the development of her own brand of personal power. She was adopted at birth, but she eventually found her birth mother, who, despite her mental illness, is now part of Marissa's life. She has also located her birth siblings, aunts, and uncles, and she has struggled to identify her birth father in the murky world in which he lived.

This reconnection with her birth family led her to make peace with her adoptive parents, too. That relationship wasn't devoid of challenges: her father is an alcoholic, her mother suffered a stroke, and Marissa was her mother's caregiver until her mother died when Marissa was only fourteen.

Marissa grew up, married, and had two children, but ultimately divorced because her husband was abusive. She has a successful career now as well as a wonderful second marriage.

But does she see herself as a hero in her own story? Does she relish the strengths she has honed as a result of the challenges she experienced? That was just not part of how she saw herself. Instead, Marissa focused on how *others* saw her—as abrasive, too direct, and aggressive—and this concerned her. Her girly thoughts were alive and well.

Are You Your Own Worst Enemy?

I found Marissa's story fascinating because even though she was doing so much to take care of herself and forge a path of self-care amid an admittedly unfair number of setbacks and roadblocks, even though today she is successful and has joy in her life, she is still her own worst enemy. Her self-directed energy, the energy she spent thinking about herself, was clearly spent criticizing herself, focusing on what others saw as deficits—all girly thoughts— instead of at least balancing this by recognizing how she had beaten the odds through the force of her personal power, her resilience.

Marissa doesn't see her own heroism in her life—how she leapt to the defense of others, how she protected not only herself but also her children from her abusive husband. She took for granted the complex task of creating a new family with her children, her birth parents, and her adoptive father. She adeptly forged a relationship with her birth father while not falling prey to his criminal involvement. She figured out how to attend college as a working mother, established herself in a very competitive career, and avoided the bad guys she felt herself drawn to romantically by marrying one of the good guys the second time around.

Yet instead of giving herself credit for doing all this, she did what her *girly thoughts* taught her to do: she saw herself as lucky rather than as determined, attributing her success to something random and external rather than to her own efforts. She focused her energy on how her abrasive personality was a problem for others, a theme she kept returning to during our first lunch. Of course, I don't see her that way, and I'm sure I'm not alone.

Your Remarkable Strength

The fact that Marissa was able to convert the adversity she experienced into personal strengths (such as her persistence) is remarkable, but it is not unique. You too have remarkable strengths that have been honed by how you've learned to deal with the adversities in your life. The key is not just to develop your resiliency but also to use this inner strength *consciously* to fight those girly thoughts. Let's explore what keeps you from using your hard-earned skills— your resilience—to assist yourself. What are you doing that is getting in the way of seeing yourself as heroic? Why don't you appreciate yourself as much as others do?

The Price You Pay

If you are going to do incredible things, if you are so very capable of caring for others, of changing yourself and your world, why do you also have to look really good in a very particular, socially condoned way?

Why do you feel so disempowered by an acne breakout, a bad hair day, or a new wrinkle?

Why do you feel the need to hide when these occur and thereby miss school, reschedule an important meeting, or turn down a date? Is your behavior a direct result of that pimple, or is it a result of the power you give various pimples (in all their guises in your life) to define your worth?

When you approach it this way, it does seem pretty ridiculous. So the question is, why do we do this? Why do we diminish our own personal power? The answer is that we sabotage ourselves through our girly thoughts.

Whether you're in the boardroom or the classroom, your girly thoughts exert an influence in your life, exacting a price that you're not even aware you are paying as you are driven to believe that to be acceptable, you must be perfect. And it's an all-or-nothing game, because girly thoughts are pervasive, unconscious, and so much a part of our culture. Here are some examples:

- **Leadership.** Do you wait to be recognized in a meeting? Do you think you have to prove yourself before you ask for a raise because you don't want to appear to be aggressive or pushy?
- **Dating.** Do you think you can't make the first move or you'll scare him away?
- **Female acquaintances.** Do you constantly check out other women to see how you measure up at work and in your community?
- **Girlfriends.** Are you the one who has to have the answer to your friends' ongoing boyfriend problems?
- **Parenting.** Do you have to be the perfect mother to be a good mother?
- **Marriage.** Are cooking, cleaning, laundry, and other household chores your second shift?
- **Parents.** Does the care and well-being of your parents fall to you because your siblings and other relatives see you as the most capable?

- **Yourself.** When you look in the mirror, do you obsess about your face, what's on it, what it needs, how it looks, how to cover your wrinkles and under-eye circles? Are you preoccupied with your weight?

The Risk of Appearing Undesirable

For many women, being seen as strong means risking being seen as unfeminine and therefore undesirable. Wonder Woman sees herself as strong, but then she doesn't have girly thoughts. Very subtle societal pressures still play out the notion that men are supposed to be the strong ones and women are supposed to be appreciative of their strength; we're supposed to need them and need to be rescued; we're not supposed to be threatening by appearing to be tough and independent. As a result, even though your own personal power is present, you tend to not be conscious of its presence and thus are unable to access it. So to embrace your personal power means to risk not being so desirable.

If Wonder Woman can do it, why can't you? When you're willing to risk being seen as something other than desirable, you free yourself to re-create your desirability. What do you want to be wanted *for*? What do you want others to notice and desire about you? Maybe you decide to age naturally and not have plastic surgery. Perhaps the ten pounds you keep losing and regaining can just sit comfortably on your frame.

So stop blaming yourself. Your girly thoughts are not your fault. You have them, but you didn't create them. In fact, in some ways you've been brainwashed into feeling the way you do. Your girly thoughts are the result of many things, including your family and

live in, where women must be perfect to be
know how easy that is to pull off!

Strength Is Beautiful

You don't have to indulge your girly thoughts. Even Wonder Woman occasionally struggled with her strength, but this didn't result in her doubting herself, and she didn't walk around concerned about her beauty. My new friend Marissa, like Wonder Woman, could be described as gorgeous, even exotic. Marissa grew up thinking she was Italian, but after connecting with her birth parents, she learned that she is part Navajo, part Irish, and even a little Chinese. She is fifty-five, tall, and striking in the way of women who are natural and powerful and don't spend much time trying to be beautiful. She is stunning because much of her beauty comes from inside—from who she is, not how she crafts herself.

This is a distinction made by Lupita Nyong'o, who was voted Most Beautiful Person of the Year by *People* magazine. Lupita, who won the Oscar for Best Supporting Actress for her portrayal of a slave in the film *12 Years a Slave*, shared what her mother told her: "Beauty can't sustain you. You can't eat beauty. . . . What does sustain us . . . what is fundamentally beautiful is compassion for yourself and for those around you. That kind of beauty enflames the heart and enchants the soul" (Butler, 2014).

You: Superheroine

You don't think you're heroic? Think again. Your girly thoughts keep you from seeing this. When you don't give in to your girly thoughts, you are so very capable of greatness.

Then do this exercise to begin to see your own heroism. In your journal, write at least one example of something you do that fulfills each statement:

- I do what needs to be done.
- I have courage and make myself act even when I'm frightened of the outcome, whether I'm asking for a raise, speaking to my child's teacher, changing a flat tire, or speaking up in a meeting.
- I can be like a mother lion when it comes to protecting those I love.
- I have perseverance. I keep working at something to get it right, even if the solution eludes me.
- I have spirit. I keep my family going when everyone else is ready to give up.
- I challenge myself to be my best, even when I don't feel that my best is nearby.
- I have faith. I believe in myself because I can learn from my mistakes.

Take a look at your answers. Do they begin to paint a different picture of you? Perhaps a you who is spunkier, more flexible, and more powerful? Someone who is not so controlled by girly thoughts?

Your Personal Kryptonite

Remember, like Superman's kryptonite, your girly thoughts disempower you. The closer you get to them, the more lethal they are. The more space they take up in you, the less space is available for the real you.

Just like kryptonite, your girly thoughts lurk in places that aren't always obvious, which is why you need practice in understanding, hearing, and noticing when these thoughts are speaking to you and triggering your unhelpful responses. You can learn to say no to this toxic self-talk and to say yes to your personal power.

In Wonder Woman's own words: "A new journey to be started. A new promise to be fulfilled. A new page to be written. Go forth unto this waiting world with pen in hand, all you young scribes, the open book awaits. Be creative. Be adventurous. Be original" (*Wonder Woman* #62 by George Perez).

DO'S & DON'TS

✓ Do enjoy identifying your favorite female superheroes.

✓ Do notice the characteristics you share with your superheroes.

✓ Do notice how your caring for others may interfere with caring for yourself.

✓ Do notice your remarkable strengths.

✓ Do notice when your *perfect* becomes the enemy of your *good*.

✗ Don't continue to be your own worst enemy.

✗ Don't continue to disempower yourself by listening to your girly thoughts.

All in the (Original) Family: Leading Yourself to Relative Success

"Grandmother," asked a young girl, "please help me.
Inside me is a terrible fight between two wolves.
One is full of love, empathy, and faith and sees the
best in others and in myself. The other is angry,
jealous, full of self-pity, inferiority, and guilt.
Tell me, Grandmother, which one will win?"
Her grandmother looked at her with knowing eyes
and answered, "The one you feed."

—Cherokee legend

Heirlooms we don't have in our family.
But stories we've got.

—Rose Cherin

As you get ready to begin your actual detox, you need to stop for a moment and consider how you arrived here. You're at a point

45

where you realize you need to change your thinking pretty radically. In the following days of the program you will explore the role of several factors that have shaped your understanding of being a woman, but one influence stands out above all others: your family, your initial template for understanding the expectations and pressures you currently feel and the solutions you currently use.

You are a product of your family, and whether you fully accepted its teachings or pushed against its teachings and produced your own beliefs, you internalized what you learned. In this chapter, we will explore what you learned and begin to consider how to change this.

How You Feed Your Girly Thoughts

You've unconsciously kept your emphasis on what is wrong with you and have thereby fed the wolf with uncertainty, inferiority, and even self-pity. This is the wolf that can move you toward seeing yourself as a victim by keeping your focus on what you do that causes others to treat you poorly, that results in spending your precious energy concentrating on what is *wrong* with you. This is the wolf that feeds your girly thoughts.

But you can change this. You can feed the wolf that nourishes your personal power, sees the best in you and in others, and is full of love and empathy.

Which Part of You Have You Been Taught to Feed?

Sooji remembers her mother saying to her, "Why do you torture yourself with these thoughts? They are hurting you. Put them out of your mind!" She also remembers thinking, *But you helped put them in my mind.*

This is the dilemma we have with our girly thoughts and the conflict we have with the women in our families who unconsciously feed them. Answer these questions to see if you were taught to put your attention on what is wrong with you:

- Was someone always correcting you—for instance, how you sat or how you dressed? Did it feel like you weren't cut any slack?
- Were you cautioned to be thin? Did anyone imply you would be undesirable if you were not?
- Were you taught that other women are a threat, always trying to take your man from you?
- Were you taught to be quiet and not question?
- Were you given the impression that older women are not desirable?
- Were you taught that sex is dirty?
- Were female bosses laughed at for their weakness?
- Were you taught that you had to please the head of the household?
- Were you taught not to flaunt your accomplishments?
- Were you rewarded for caring for others and sacrificing yourself?
- Were you taught that you didn't really understand money?
- Was parenting the one job you were encouraged to take?

These questions represent the messages that are the basis for several of our girly thoughts, and most of us can answer yes to many of them.

Here are some additional questions to ask yourself about how

you were taught to spend your energy on developing your personal
power, your resilience:

- Did you feel loved?
- Did you feel accepted no matter what your weight was or
  how your body looked?
- Were you helped to make friends and see past the limitations
  of others?
- Was your opinion valued?
- Were your accomplishments celebrated?
- Were female elders in your family respected?
- Were you taught to respect *all* adults?
- Were you taught to give yourself an "attagirl" for your personal
  achievements?

Mom: Your Primary Girly Thoughts Instructor

When you were a child and painted a picture of your mother,
you would use bright, primary, and maybe even clashing colors.
Somehow, there was nothing neutral about Mom. As we grow and
age, we hear her voice, and we use her as our principal role model.

Your mother remains the most important influence on the
woman you are, girly thoughts and all. As much as we love our
mothers and as much as we admire their strength, compassion,
wisdom, and high tolerance for stress, few of us want to be our
mothers. We have witnessed how much the constraints of society's
gender roles limited her. We witnessed the pain she experienced
because of the traditional social restrictions on women, we saw
how she was able to triumph in spite of them, and we promised
ourselves never to be in her position. Whether we were born of our

mothers' bodies or adopted and born of their hearts, our mothers represented our first model of what being a woman entailed.

Remember that your mother also had a mother. Your intergenerational legacy of what it means to be a woman and how a woman should act is strong.

Like Mother, Like Daughter

When our mothers look at us, they also see themselves: their hopes, dreams, and fears. They don't want us to repeat their mistakes. They fear us growing away from them, yet they long for us to be free.

When your mother looks at you, do you ever wonder what she sees? In her multigenerational novel *The Joy Luck Club*, Amy Tan (1989) described the look that women give younger women who are their daughters' ages: "In me," said one of these younger women, "they see their own daughters, just as ignorant, just as unmindful of all the truths and hopes." Perhaps this is why our mothers tend to hover, why they are so concerned that we not make the mistakes that they did, why they are fearful that we will follow their scripts instead of creating our own.

Girly thoughts are pretty exacting and have clear consequences. They are passed down from one generation to the next, mother to daughter, and reinforced by grandmothers and aunts, not to mention the media and literature. Is it any wonder that women have such complicated relationships with the women in their families?

See Your Mother for the Girl She Was

Based on your mother's challenges, she drew certain conclusions about herself, her life, and her role as a woman. This formed the basis for what she taught you, and it's important for you to understand so you can begin to know her and eventually make peace with her about how she raised you to be a woman. From what you know about your mother, from what you have concluded from your lifelong study of her words and actions, answer the following questions:

- How did your mother feel about herself as a woman?
- How did your mother see herself compared to other women?
- Did your mother feel constrained in her life?
- What were your mother's girly thoughts?
- How did you see her limited in her life?

Family Stories

Your mother wasn't the only person who helped you learn the lessons that became girly thoughts—she had plenty of help from her contemporaries and her ancestors. Your mother and other family members used family stories to get their points across.

Think about it. What do we do at a family gathering? We all share stories of that rich complex undertaking called life. Often, these stories are about the things we find funny, objectionable, or unbelievable. But what is *in* the story is something else again. This is where the true teaching occurs—girly thoughts are taught through the lessons learned in the family and shared in our family tales.

It is in these lessons that the identity of the family is established. Your role as a woman was told not just once but over and over through the stories you heard as a child and through the stories you continue to share about yourself. These are subtle (and sometimes not-so-subtle) reminders of your family's expectations of you and how you either fulfilled them or did not.

Millie remembers her mother always telling stories about how proud Grandma was that she was a mother. As a single lesbian in her late forties, Millie always felt these stories as a jab.

Amber, who always had weight issues, was reminded again and again about "not letting herself go" as so many women in her family had done.

Morgan, who was recently divorced, felt wounded when her mother spoke of the strong tradition of women in their family "keeping the family together."

Breeding Ground for Girly Thoughts

Let's look at two major family themes that are found in your family stories and are told so often that they find their way into how you judge yourself. These themes are the breeding ground for your girly thoughts. The first one is uniquely female; the second strikes at the core of how we treat ourselves.

The Green-Eyed Monster

Your mother's insecurities weighed heavily on her, as yours do on you. One way these insecurities are expressed intergenerationally is through teaching women to be wary of each other. This message pits women against each other in a variety of settings from work to intimate relationships, setting up jealous rivalries. Women see other women as competition, both for the scarce resource of men and for the power position in an organization, the queen bee spot.

Do you think this rivalry isn't currently going on in your life? Ask yourself the following:

- When you go to a party, for whom do you dress?
- Do you notice the attention other women give your husband, boyfriend, or partner?

- Do you check out the clothing and actions of other women at work?

How Love Was Shown

This theme hits everyone in the family, but when being loved is a central theme in your girly thoughts, you were hit particularly hard. Every family has a unique way of showing love, including cues that are readily understandable to those who are members but are a mystery to those who haven't been schooled in these interpretations. Here are some examples:

- You worked hard to receive good grades so you could earn a small smile of approval from your father.
- Your mother showed her love for her family by keeping a clean house or cooking intricate meals because she didn't have a career outside the home.
- Your new mother-in-law views her criticism of your accessories as a sign of involvement in bringing you up to the family standards and therefore as a sign of love.
- Your aunt lets you in on the "secret" that nobody in the family approves of your brother's wife; secrets like this are shared only with loved and trusted family members.
- Although your grandparents never had two nice words to say to each other in your presence, you are told how much they loved each other because they stayed together despite so many years of discord.

Each family shows love in a variety ways, and each of us is schooled on interpretation. This translates into how we show love and how our girly thoughts insist that love must be demonstrated.

This limited lens can be painful and even crippling in an intimate relationship.

Raine recalls the intense fights she would have with Jeb because she believed he didn't love her:

> In my family, my father would beat me and then say, "I wouldn't do this if I didn't love you." With Jeb, I kept insisting that he didn't love me, and we'd end up in these heated arguments with lots of tears, and then he'd just hold me. I later realized that for me, love was the making up after the fight. If he could stand by me after I had lost it, then he loved me. After all, this was the model for love my father used.

What Your Girly Thoughts Tell You
About Being Loved

Consider what you have learned in your family about love and how these beliefs have translated into what your girly thoughts are telling you about love:

- Do you have to be perfect to be loved?
- If you make a big mistake, will you suffer total rejection?
- Is love so fragile that you have to keep testing it to see whether it is still there?
- Do you need to earn love by all the things you do for others?
- Do you need to be sexually attractive to be loved?
- Do you need to do more than your partner because you are essentially defective in some way?
- Do you need to join in with disapproving family members who are bullying another in order to be accepted and loved?

The actual messages you learned are contained in how your family helped you to script your life, and you internalized these into your girly thoughts.

Stop Living Your Girly Thoughts Script

Over time, you formed a type of script for living—a girly thoughts script that sees cause and effect in a certain way and teaches you how to fulfill your part as a woman.

Once you understand the power of your family stories, you can have some fun. *Changing the message can be as simple as changing the emphasis, sometimes changing the lesson that is at the end of the story.* This will require a little effort, but the nice thing about family stories is that you are bound to get lots of practice doing this.

How do you go about changing the script based on your family stories? Try these suggestions:

- Listen for the rationalization that the poor behavior of another was the woman's fault—that is a girly thought. Uncle Sam's affair was a result of Aunt Alice gaining weight. Cousin Carol decided to go back to work even though her kids were not yet in school and even though her husband would feel "like less of a man." Your sister's decision to put career first cost her her marriage. These are all girly thoughts.
- Consider challenging those conclusions.
- Consider offering an alternative way of viewing the circumstances.
- Consider pointing out the strength needed by the woman to make the choice she made.

Over time you will be able not only to challenge your family's viewpoints but also to begin to change how your family sees the women involved—yourself included. In *Your Life Calling: Reimagining the Rest of Your Life,* Jane Pauley wrote, "The secret to reinvention is that there isn't one" (2014). She's right. It just requires that you desire to change your thinking.

Your family is your first and arguably your most influential teacher in this wonderful adventure called life. But your family is not your only teacher. In the next part of the detox plan, you will examine different domains of your life to learn how your toxic girly thoughts are affecting you and to determine how to change this. Regardless of the amount of influence your family of origin had or continues to have, you'll be able to answer for yourself what you need to do to detox from your girly thoughts—this miserable way of thinking in your own life.

DO'S & DON'TS

✓ Do know that your family is just your beginning—
the end is up to you.

✓ Do feed the wolf that brings out your finest qualities.

✓ Do have fun helping your family fine-tune its identity.

✓ Do follow the best in your family's teachings.

✗ Don't blame your mother for being the best girl in her
family that she could be.

✗ Don't blame your mother for the challenges she
experienced as a woman.

Detox Summary for Part I

Fully Seeing Yourself

To be fully seen by somebody, then,
and be loved anyhow—this is a human offering
that can border on miraculous.

—Elizabeth Gilbert

If you want the rainbow, you've got
to put up with the rain.

—Dolly Parton

You have embarked on this journey by beginning to get to know the miracle that is you. Let's look at what you have found that is getting in the way. Summarize the life script that includes your girly thoughts.

Women from my family have been taught to:

1. _____

2. _____

3. _____

Now it's time to change these. Let's keep it simple. Think about what you've just read and written down and answer the following:

• What excites you about changing your girly thoughts?
• List a specific belief you will target for challenging now.

- Specify new ways of thinking about yourself that you will culti-vate to replace this girly thought, even if it feels like a stretch.
- Consider what specific support you will need to accomplish this.
- Have fun listing the experimental actions you will take.
- Begin the practice of writing and saying positive affirmations when you're thinking a girly thought to help you move past it. Post the affirmations on sticky notes in obvious spots, such as on your computer or your bathroom mirror, as you explore new ways of speaking about yourself. For example:
  - ➤ That's not me, that's my girly thought talking.
  - ➤ I'm a funny and complicated woman full of girly thoughts; I'm not crazy.
  - ➤ I come from a pretty interesting family; it's good I'm figuring me out.

Remember to notice your successes as you begin to detox from your girly thoughts, your negative habitual thinking about your-self. Jot down how you are making changes, and share these obser-vations with a trusted friend.

Next you will explore your thoughts and feelings about yourself on a very intimate level.

PART II

DETOXING IN YOUR INTIMATE LIFE: How Your Girly Thoughts Affect You Personally

*Step away from the Mean Girls . . . and say
bye-bye to feeling bad about your looks. Are you
ready to stop colluding with a culture that makes so
many of us feel physically inadequate? . . . Just look into
the mirror and see your face. When the criticism
drops away, what you will see then is just you,
without judgment, and that is the first step toward
transforming your experience of the world.*

—Oprah Winfrey

Courage is like a muscle. We strengthen it by use.

—Ruth Gordon

You are now ready to begin your detox in earnest. For each of the next eight days, you will first complete an exercise to help you identify the specific girly thoughts you're having in a particular area. Next you'll be guided in understanding how you got here and what you can do to change this toxic thought. Finally, you'll consider new skills that you can develop as a way to expand your explorations into the new, real you after you peel away those girly thoughts.

In Part II our focus is on the intimate you: how you feel and treat your body—your sexuality, your need to be loved, and your desire to stay forever youthful. We will explore how your girly thoughts reinforce your worst feelings about yourself, instilling a lack of confidence and self-worth.

But that's only half the story. Now that you have a term to describe what this toxic inner dialogue is and how you do this to yourself with your girly thoughts, I will show you how to fight back: how to not buy into the "corporate images of beauty" (Samakow, 2014), how to change how you see yourself, how to change how you speak about yourself, and what you want to project into this, the most personal part of your life.

Change Your Thinking, Change Your Life

Remember to describe the various ways you are changing your life every day in your journal. Write down not just the exercises and your related thoughts but also the random "aha!" moments you are bound to have as you go through your day.

As you get ready to consider the sources of your self-limiting girly thoughts over the next eight days, remember that you are worth the time it will take to do this. You are about to embark on a life-changing exploration that will lead you to change how you look at yourself and the world around you and how you value yourself.

You will develop strategies for challenging your girly thoughts, keeping in mind an African proverb: It is not what you call me; it is what I answer to that matters.

Let's begin Part II, where I will teach you how to answer to your true self, not your girly thoughts.

You *Are* So Beautiful: Choosing Self-Love Over Self-Judgment

*Beauty is in the eye of the beholder, and
it may be necessary from time to time to give a
stupid or misinformed beholder a black eye.*

—Miss Piggy

*The Victorian woman became her ovaries, as
today's woman has become her "beauty."*

—Naomi Wolf

Beauty is whatever gives joy.

—Edna St. Vincent Millay

Today's Detox Goal: See Your Own Beauty

Would you post a nude picture of yourself on Facebook? Is posting a nude picture of yourself on Facebook ever a good idea? NO . . . but even if this thought did cross your mind, would you think of doing so after the birth of your child, even if all vital parts were covered? "In May 2013, Taryn Brumfitt, an Australian body builder, [a] recent mother, and [a] founder of the Body Image Movement, posted a before-and-after photo on Facebook that received more than 3 million 'likes' . . . but the side-by-side comparison wasn't showing off a post-weight loss flat stomach. The 'before' shot was taken at [a] body building contest, and the 'after' was post-birth." Why? "Because heaven forbid a woman can love her body after [giving birth]," Brumfitt said (Samakow, 2014).

Mirror, Mirror on the Wall, Who's the Fairest of Them All?

If your answer to the fairy-tale question in the heading above isn't you, then your girly thoughts are working their poison and draining you of your confidence. Begin a new page in your journal, and let's see what's going on:

- When you look in the mirror, what part of your body do you see first?
- Is this your favorite part? If not, then why does your attention go there first?
- What do you think as you look at this part of you?
- Are you pleased by this thought? Is it helpful to you?

Repeat this process and answer these questions as you look at the next part of your body. Then do the next, and the next, and keep going until you get the picture of how you are treating yourself.

So, how do you feel about your body? Don't hold back here—
let's get it all out.

Beauty Is in the Eye of the Beholder

We are so judgmental of what we see when we look in a mirror.
Many women give themselves what feels like a slap in the face when
they behold their own image, and they either become obsessed
with "fixing" whatever they perceive as flaws or tend to just give
up, citing not enough time or money to take care of themselves.

So what exactly do you want? To be someone else? Good luck
with that, even if you do buy Wonderbras, Spanx, and the "right"
creams and makeup; work out like crazy; and buy into the latest
fad diet.

Feminist writer Annie Roiphe (2014) says, "A woman whose
smile is open and whose expression is glad has a kind of beauty
no matter what she wears." So why is it so frightening for you to
see yourself as beautiful? When you look at yourself in the mirror,
two things occur:

1. You see not only how you look but also many other parts
   of who you are, and they are all so emotionally loaded.
2. You compare yourself to the digital image of perfection
   hat surrounds you in the media.

These are both big issues that we'll revisit on subsequent detox
days. As you'll learn, your girly thoughts and their sources are
all interrelated, but they are born and developed by some strong
influences you may not have even considered. When you look in
the mirror, you see the following:

- Expectations of others, particularly your mother
- The part of you that is like your ancestors (even if you were adopted and do not know your ancestors directly)
- Who you were in your childhood and youth
- Who you are today
- Who you are afraid to be

Many women struggle with their looks, particularly in relation to their weight. Show me a woman who doesn't think she could afford to lose at least five pounds, and I'll show you a woman who has conquered her girly thoughts. That woman can and will be *you*! Let's begin your detox by tackling several common body image issues.

Girly Thought #1: I'm Fat

Author Elizabeth Gilbert wrote, "In all the years that you have . . . undressed in front of a gentleman has he ever asked you to leave? Has he ever walked out and left? No? It's because he doesn't care! He's in a room with a naked girl, he just won the lottery" (2013).

Think about that for a moment and then ask yourself, *So who has the problem here?* Then ask yourself the following:

- Do you tuck in your tummy each time you look in the mirror?
- Do you buy magazines with the latest quick diet ("Lose 10 Pounds in 7 Days!") listed on the cover?
- Do you keep dieting and gaining the weight back?
- Do you attribute many of the bad things that happen to you to your weight?

- Have you used apps like SkinneePix, which promises to shave fifteen pounds off your selfies?

Do you see how your obsession with being thin is costing you your self-esteem? Naomi Wolf (2002) wrote in *The Beauty Myth*, "A cultural fixation on female thinness is not an obsession about female beauty but an obsession about female obedience." And this is obedience to the cultural messages in our girly thoughts.

The issue is not how to lose weight, but why doing so is so important—such an obsession, even—for so many women. The answer is that your girly thoughts tell you that your worth is tied to your weight. The reasoning goes something like this: "Young women are more desirable; young women are thin. I need to be thin if I am going to be desirable." So you starve yourself, or you eat and purge, and you plan to exercise.

The second half of this plan—exercise—presents a significant challenge for women. Exercise means making time for yourself. And time—well, as Michelle Obama says, "We need to do a better job of putting ourselves higher on our own 'to do' list" (Lepore, 2014). This has resulted in some predictable ways that we reinforce our toxic inner dialogue about being too fat.

The Source: The Myth of the Quick Diet Fix

I recently addressed a group of very powerful female executives about girly thoughts. When I spoke of how to really lose weight, the room became absolutely still. I said, "You all know how to lose weight." All eyes were on me. I gave them the answer: "You eat less and exercise more." The women sighed and laughed; the tension was broken, and they realized there was no quick answer here.

Make a quick list of all the diet plans you've tried:

1. _____

2. _____

3. _____

Now go back and write a few sentences about the results.

Enter the New Year's resolution. Here you have the opportunity to begin anew, to make conscious decisions that will improve your life—and for many of us, this is to lose weight, especially the weight we just gained over the holidays. Instead it turns into your annual way of feeling really bad about yourself.

Goals are good. There is nothing wrong with having weight loss as a goal, but the way you go about fulfilling this particular goal will determine whether you have a great year or another year in which you start out strong, fizzle out fast, and then beat yourself up.

Your desire to lose weight is just what the multibillion-dollar diet industry has been waiting for. You are reminded to try the latest quick-loss diet plan through ads on TV and by magazines at the grocery checkout counter (as you're also tempted by the most delicious-looking desserts on the covers of some of the same magazines). But will that newest plan really work for you, particularly when other plans haven't? Maybe it's time to look deeper at what caused your weight gain in the first place.

Are you like thirty-two-year-old Veronica, who eats and drinks all she wants during the holidays? Like her, do you begin a diet in the new year and then feel depressed because you don't lose the weight quickly? "I used to somewhat manage my holiday weight gain," Veronica shared, "but after I had my daughter and then my son, it just didn't work. My weight kept creeping up. I tried every new diet, all with disappointing results. I just went into a funk, feeling my body was betraying me."

Consider now a New Year's resolution that will actually enable you to feel better about yourself. How about committing to stop the toxic inner dialogue about your body?

The Plan: Lose Some Stress

Stress can be a significant factor in weight gain. Those extra pounds did not come from nowhere. You are probably a stress eater. This means that when you feel stress, you do something to relieve it, and that may mean eating or drinking to calm down.

When you feel stressed, you feel deserving of that brownie; it has your name on it, doesn't it? After all, *desserts* is just *stressed* spelled backward!

Consider these scenarios:

- You've having a really bad day at work. You deserve a 3:00 PM candy bar, and that chocolate does send you to another place.
- As part of the eating frenzy that is a family dinner, your kids want spaghetti—seconds, even. And if they're going to have seconds, you might as well, too. Why not, since you're overweight anyway?
- It's finally Saturday night, and there should be time for *you*. But a report is due Monday morning, so there goes your quiet night. You might as well dig into a new bag of chips while you work.

Sound familiar? Let's get to the bottom of your own stress-eating issues. First, list when and where you stress-eat.

1. _____

2. _____

3. _____

Now go back and quickly write down everything you *could* do other than eat the next time you feel stressed. Are you having a hard time with this? Think of things that will make you feel better:

- A hug
- A walk
- A glass of cool water
- A sexual fantasy
- Looking at the sky and realizing that whatever is stressing you will at some point be over

Dieting Stresses You Even More

Stress is a given in your life. But to lose it or reduce it, you need to figure out what is stressing you. If you are a stress eater—that is, if you eat as a way to calm yourself—dieting only increases your stress because you are taking away your major stress reducer. This is why diets do not work. Dieting increases your stress. You are now in a no-win situation.

The Stress of Girly Thoughts

A strategy with an even bigger payoff and no back-end payout is to reduce your stress level. And what stresses women out is all those societal messages—those girly thoughts—that tell you the following:

- You're too fat.
- You're too young.

- You're too old.
- Your hips are too big.
- Your breasts are sagging.

Is it any surprise that you take solace in something that gives you immediate satisfaction, like eating or drinking? But what if there were something you could do that would accomplish the same thing—calm you down and give you satisfaction—with no calories?

The Solution: Challenge Your Stressful Girly Thoughts— A Zero-Calorie Solution

Learning to talk back to the negative inner dialogue where your girly thoughts are found is one way to do that. How does this work?

Identify the Cause(s) of Your Stress

If your stress is caused by your girly thoughts, then name them. Naming something for what it is gives us power over it. Instead of thinking that your weight has something to do with your husband attending so many evening meetings, realize that you are blaming yourself for his actions, and that this is another girly thought.

Don't Let a Thought Determine How You Feel

Don't buy into *if this, then that*. Having a negative girly thought— or any negative thought, for that matter—does not have to determine how you feel. It is, after all, just a thought.

Tell Your Girly Thoughts to Take a Hike

None of us can control what pops into our minds, but we can control what we allow to be there rent-free. You choose whether to indulge a negative thought about yourself. And if you decide not to go there, instead you can do the following:

- Tell your girly thoughts to get lost.
- Treat each girly thought lightly, thanking it for its wisdom but saying you're not interested.
- Invite yourself to think of something else, something more pleasant, such as a massage, sitting on the beach, sex, or hugging your baby.

Name Your Stress Triggers

List the stresses that cause you to go on the see-food diet:

1. _____

2. _____

3. _____

Being aware of your triggers for stress eating is helpful so you can isolate them, think self-loving thoughts, and take positive actions. Go back over your list, and to each stressor add a self-loving statement.

You can control what you think, and by doing so you can reduce your stress, cut down on your stress eating and drinking, and save some money on all those worthless diet books that you rarely read anyway.

So to really lose weight, stop thinking those girly thoughts by identifying the thought, understanding where it's coming from, and replacing it with self-loving thoughts and actions. That's the essence of detoxing from any girly thought.

Girly Thought #2: I Hate My Body Because I Don't Look Like a Model or a Movie Star

Hate is a strong word, and I use it purposefully. The truth is that we do at times hate our looks. This is *not* helpful. This self-hatred causes you to punish yourself and be mean to yourself because you're so angry that you are not the current ideal (which you know keeps changing).

Let's look at some ways you may be doing this:

- Do you buy beauty magazines and then imitate the model's pout or stance as you try to look like her—even if you are only five foot one?
- Do you try to copy the way celebrities dress, only to be disappointed when something doesn't come in your size or doesn't look good on you?
- Do you worry because you don't have flawless skin like the models and actresses you admire?
- Do you worry about parts of your body that do not conform to the current beauty standards, bemoaning that you wear glasses or have pendulous breasts, a flat chest, short legs, thin lips, or a large nose?
- Do you feel too old to be attractive?

Answering yes to any of these questions tells you that you are seeing and judging yourself through the lens of your girly thoughts.

The Source: Photoshop, Special Lighting, and Theatrical Makeup

Celebrities look different in real life, as we can see in the "gotcha" publications at every supermarket's checkout lines. During a radio interview, a model recently shared with me, "I think I've been having girly thoughts. I wake up in the morning and look at myself in the mirror, and I feel sad because I don't look like me." She was equating the altered images of her with the real her, and she found the difference between the two depressing. I too felt sad hearing what she was doing to herself. *This is crazy*, I thought, yet this is what women tell me they are doing to themselves every day. Let's counter this impulse to see others as beautiful and you as lacking.

The Plan: See Real Women's Real Bodies

Models and celebrities may be gorgeous women, but they are flesh and blood, with all the imperfections that come with this. In real life they are not polished or sculpted. In real life, they, like you, are beautiful women with pores, cellulite, and even wrinkles (Pipher and Kilbourne, 2000). The difference is that their *job* is to look gorgeous, and in the words of actress Sandra Bullock, it takes a team to create the public her. Your job may be to be a student, an office manager, or a physician; whatever you do, it is not your job to look pretty, so you don't have a team working on your makeup and your hair and a daily personal trainer supervising your workouts and your diet.

Now it's time to deconstruct your girly thoughts by becoming an educated consumer. Find a copy or two of your favorite fashion magazine, or find images online, and pick out three or four ads that really bother you because the models are just too polished.

Tear out the print images or print the online images and put them in your journal.

Pay special attention to the model. Ask yourself some basic questions, such as the following:

- Does her skin have pores?
- Is her waist impossibly small?
- Are her legs impossibly long?

Read my blog on Photoshop at *http://thepowerfulwoman.net/ digital-dreams-girly-thoughts/.lose weight*

Realize that you are not competing with a real woman; these images are enhanced to create perfection. When you aspire to look like those women, you are not aspiring to look like a real person. The images that surround us are of women who are so heavily made up, so altered, that they more closely resemble a fun-house image: a distortion of the real image, but in this case, distorted in a socially idealized way.

Now have some fun. Contact the product manufacturer or the magazine and share your thoughts. Your letter doesn't have to be perfectly written, but do share how you feel about seeing this *manufactured* woman. Don't worry—you don't have to send the letter if you really don't want to. Let these images inspire instead of frustrate you. Use your annoyance to motivate you to change—not a fake, Photoshop picture change, but real and beneficial change.

The Solution: Appreciate Your Beauty

As you consider your own body and how you think about beauty, think about how great beauty has been created. Beauty is so much more than how you look on the outside.

When the sculptor Michelangelo was complimented on carving the beautiful statue of David, he said that all he did was to bring out the beauty that was already in the stone. You are like that stone: a thing of beauty just waiting to be revealed.

Bring Out Your Inner Beauty

Rather than thinking that you need to *make* yourself beautiful by putting on makeup, wearing Spanx, or getting breast implants, think about bringing out your inner beauty. I'm not suggesting you shouldn't do those things if they make you feel better; I am suggesting that you focus on your internal beauty instead of just your physical appearance.

Is the idea of bringing out the beauty that is already within you a different perspective for you? What would happen if you decided to bring out the beauty that is already in you rather than focusing on ways to create the beauty you want others to see? Accomplishing this involves similar steps but different goals:

- The goal for bringing out your internal beauty is discovering and honoring who you are.
- The goal for focusing on your external beauty is projecting an image that appeals to what you think others find attractive.

Which would be more fulfilling to you?

Have Fun with Your Beauty

"Do a body blessing every night before you go to sleep. Close your eyes and scan through your body parts, starting at the top of your head and working downward. As you approach each body part, pay attention to any negative thoughts that come into your mind, such as 'I hate my big backside.' Turn it around into an affirmation, such as 'Thank you, Bottom, for cushioning me when I sit.' Do this all the way down to your toes" (Rankin, 2009).

Remind Yourself of the Reality

Every time you see a Photoshopped picture, tell yourself, *It is her job to look beautiful. Even this photo of her is not real. In contrast, I've brought out my true beauty.*

DO'S & DON'TS

✓ Do get to explore, know, and appreciate each and every part of your body.

✓ Do walk around feeling beautiful every day.

✓ Do have some fun and point out Photoshop images to your friends and your family members.

✗ Don't buy into girly thoughts that have you scrutinizing yourself for "imperfections."

✗ Don't starve yourself to feel better.

✓ Do bring out your inner beauty, today.

Sex: A No-Judgment Zone

No woman gets an orgasm from
shining the kitchen floor.

—Betty Friedan

Man may have discovered fire, but women
discovered how to play with it.

—Candace Bushnell, *Sex and the City*

Sex appeal is 50 percent what you've got and
50 percent what people think you've got.

—Sophia Loren

Today's Detox Goal:
Welcome Your Sexuality

"I feel I can never win. I'm attractive. Men like to look at me, a lot. Women hate me. My boyfriend always thinks I'm having an affair, so he's angry with me. All I want to do is be successful, have friends, and enjoy my life," Maria says, sighing.

For Women, Liking Sex Is Like Playing with Fire

Playing with sex is like playing with fire: we're thrilled—fascinated, even—but we don't want to get burned, and that's the tricky part. Speaking about women and sex is a highly nuanced conversation. Although we are expected to be good at certain things, being good sexually does not convey the same status for women that it does for men. A man can be seen as a stud and can even be polyamorous, but can a woman?

The sexual part of who we are is definitely noticed by both men and women, even if we ourselves are not in touch with it. We are criticized by husbands or lovers if we are not sexual enough and called a slut by society if sex is too important in our lives. So to enjoy sex and be sexually fulfilled is complicated. Talk about mixed messages. Angelina Jolie once said, "I think it is funny that we were freer about sexuality in the 4th century B.C." (Morrigan, 2013). No wonder our girly thoughts have a field day with our attitudes toward sex.

Answer these two questions:

- Are you uncomfortable with your own sexuality?
- Are you uncomfortable being overtly sexual, even in private situations?

Girly Thought #3: I'm a Good Girl, and Good Girls Don't . . .

There's that good girl thought again: your need to be the fairy-tale princess and to be rescued and taken, but not to be directly sexual. Your girly thoughts are a mixed bag about this, because they tell you to love sex, but not to initiate what you find pleasurable. Hmm. Not too long ago, women who loved sex were labeled aberrant. Today, if you don't love sex, you're considered dysfunctional.

Your sexuality, like many of your other physical and emotional responses, is culturally determined. There is so much pressure on women to be sexual, but in just the right way (whatever that is), so it is a no-win situation as we try to figure this out and understand what is expected of us.

The Source: Women's Sexuality Has Been Buried and Misunderstood

There is such a history of requiring women to be seen as not sexually aggressive. Women have been told this, believed this and have been so burdened by other responsibilities that it has been difficult to be sexual (Bergner, 2013). The result is that many women suppress their sexuality.

The Plan: Explore Your Sexual Fantasies

What I am suggesting may seem almost heretical and will certainly be uncomfortable, but it is necessary. There is more to you than you allow, and your sexuality is an important part of you that you have probably minimized. Paraphrasing the words of Dr. Clarissa Pinkola Estés (1996) in her groundbreaking book *Women Who Run with the Wolves*, I encourage you to explore the parts of you that are hidden, moist, and secret in your sexual fantasies.

Rather than listening to your girly thoughts, which are full of the expectations that surround you, you will be much better off if you figure out what you need and what you want, no matter how terrifying it may be. This means you need to figure out what *you* want instead of trying to fulfill someone else's expectations. There are many ways to explore your sexual fantasies, but first you have to accept that you have them.

That brings us to the first part of your plan: permission to dream and to invent your own fantasies, even placing yourself as a character in a book, a TV show, or a movie you have enjoyed.

Permission to Fantasize

As you learned on Day 4, when women are so consumed with being beautiful and spend so much energy on what this means and how to achieve it, they spend less time on other things—like understanding their own sexuality. Sexual anthropologist Bella Ellwood-Clayton (2013) wrote that women "are too busy chasing beautiful to want to kiss beautifully. Too busy chasing the veneer of desirability to desire. Our animal instincts have become inverted: time devoted to preening overrides time devoted to mating and sexual pleasure." Our girly thoughts are directing our energy to places that are socially acceptable but not as potentially rewarding as a fulfilling sexual experience.

This brings up an important point about fantasy. Fantasy is fantasy. Thinking about a sexually stimulating scenario doesn't mean you really want to do it. There is a difference between thoughts and actions in many areas, and sex is no different. Fantasy is dreaming of punching someone whom you have no intention of actually punching or imagining yourself eating a whole chocolate cake that you know you'd never get down.

But it is fun to think about punching that jerk or eating that whole cake, and it may be fun to have your specific sexual fantasies as well. Your fantasy can free you up to have some enjoyment, to experience another level of pleasure or entertainment—even one that is outside the social norms that your girly thoughts tell you are acceptable. But the good girl in your girly thoughts may tell you that this is wrong or, worse, that your fantasies are perverted.

Research on women's sexual fantasies has shown that in controlled settings, women find a wider range of situations and scenarios sexually stimulating than men do (Bergner, 2013). Think about this. Is this different from what you would have predicted?

Think about how much fun it would be to have sex with a younger man, a woman, in a threesome, or with someone anonymous.

What are *your* sexual fantasies?

Express Your Fantasies

Women often feel ashamed of their sexual fantasies, and of course you have them. Consider why your girly thoughts have so much power over you and keep you from even knowing your sexual fantasies. Ask yourself whether your girly thoughts tell you any of the following:

- Your fantasies are too weird or disgusting.
- Your fantasies are too different.
- You'll be judged for having them.
- They will be threatening to your partner.
- They will somehow emasculate your male partner if you share them.
- You'll be forced to act on them if you allow yourself to own them.

List one or two of your fantasies in your journal. (Remember, this is *your* journal, and it's private. You don't have to share it, and I am not recommending that you share on Facebook, but it would be good to own each fantasy so you can free yourself from the constraints that say this is wrong, that good girls don't . . . [fill in the blank].) Then spend a few minutes writing the answers to these questions:

- What do your sexual fantasies tell you about yourself?
- Do your sexual fantasies raise any of the following fears that come out in your girly thoughts?
  - I am too . . . [fill in the blank].
  - Good girls don't initiate sex.
  - My sexual parts are unattractive.

I have found that women frequently have the fantasy of having sex in the kitchen! Why should this be so? Perhaps it is because women traditionally spend a great deal of creative time in that room. Molly recently shared her sexual fantasy about kitchen sex with me, but when she shared it with her husband, he was clearly uncomfortable. So they proceeded to the bedroom, where she did not particularly enjoy herself.

Are your sexual fantasies different from those of your male partner? There is only one way to find out, and that is to share them. But chances are they will be different. Wouldn't it be fun to explore both—his and yours? This doesn't mean you have to act them out. But that is the fun of fantasies: they allow us to express what's in our heads, and that is freeing. Just discussing them can be a turn-on, which Molly discovered as she persisted in sharing hers with her husband.

The Solution: Give Yourself Permission to Explore

Stop worrying about what other people might think, and give yourself permission to explore your thoughts by doing the following:

- Sketching
- Reading (Why do you think romance novels are so popular?)
- Buying intimate garments you like (hello, Victoria's Secret)
- Dressing provocatively, even if this is just for yourself
- Watching an erotic movie, even if you are comfortable only doing this by yourself
- Getting to know what type of touch you like by massaging yourself

Just thinking about your sexuality is a big step forward from listening to what your girly thoughts instruct you to do.

Girly Thought #4: I Must Keep My Partner Sexually Happy, or Else . . .

It is sad that many of our girly thoughts have an "or else" in them—in this case, "or else he'll find someone else," for example. This girly thought keeps you anxious and feeling insecure; it certainly does not put you in the mood for being sexual or enjoying sex.

Faking an Orgasm

When a woman allows her girly thoughts into her sex life, she finds herself making what is designed to be a mutually enjoyable experience into an either-or experience. For many women, pleasing a partner often means not pleasing herself. Many women deal with this by faking an orgasm. Your partner can feel that he has pleased you, which is, after all, a goal and part of his pleasure. He's happy, but are you?

Unfortunately, for many women this means ending up unsatisfied, perhaps even angry, and it contributes to shutting down sexually. Sex becomes work instead of fun. As Tasha put it, "Marital sex is another job, which I don't need at the end of the day. There's nothing in it for me, and it makes me mad. But I do it to keep him happy."

Too Tired for Sex

The fatigue experienced at the end of a very long day does play havoc with a woman's sexual feelings. Does this mean that women have a lower sex drive than men do? Or is the answer something different and more obvious? We know that sex is different for women. But no researcher is willing to say that a woman's sex drive is lower; in fact, recent research indicates that it may even be higher (Bergner, 2013). It is also more complicated.

What I have found in my clinical work with women is that there may be a more simple answer. Sex takes energy. It's certainly fun and exciting, but you also need time and attention to devote to this activity. If you are exhausted, if you feel beaten down by all the demands in your life and all the second-guessing of your girly thoughts, then at the end of the day, when you hit the bed, you want to rest. The energy for sex may not be there. Does this mean you're shut down sexually—or just exhausted? I think you know the answer to this one. Don't confuse the two. And don't let your girly thoughts take over and provide you with the worst-case scenario, which names *you* as the problem. Don't believe for a moment that you are not sexy!

This is one scenario that is often more circumstantial than physiological. Your libido is there; it's just tired.

Sex and Housework

One of the most common complaints I hear from men in couples counseling is that there is not enough sexual intimacy in the relationship. There are many reasons for this, but a common one, not often addressed, is that at the end of the workday, men and women are usually tired. Whereas a man often feels comfortable coming home and relaxing, women are coming home to their second shift: dinner, kids' homework, laundry, housecleaning. At the end of their second shift, women feel exhausted! Clara says it best: "I can't keep my eyes open, even with coffee after dinner."

Whereas a now-relaxed man may feel amorous, a pooped and maybe annoyed woman often just wants to go to sleep. The result is either perfunctory sex, which the woman doesn't find particularly enjoyable, or no sex, which begins to annoy both of them.

The Source: The Folklore That Exists on Commitment

Somehow, being committed to someone else has translated into not being committed to yourself—good girl thoughts morph into codependency. This occurs on so many levels, but nowhere as clearly as in the sexual part of a committed relationship, where somehow pleasing someone else means not pleasing yourself.

The Plan: Figure Out What Pleases You Sexually

Doesn't your partner want you to be pleased? Doesn't he or she ask you what you would like, maybe not in so many words, but

through gestures or innuendo? What is so wrong with express-
ing your desires? Your girly thoughts tell you that you need to be
concerned about how your body looks during sex or that good
girls don't initiate sex, have sexual fantasies, or ask for what they
find pleasurable. In fact, happy and fulfilled women do, and it may
be time to figure out what is on your preference list. When you
strip away the *shoulds* of your girly thoughts, you may be left with
many questions about just what works and doesn't work for you.
And if you already know the answers, then it is definitely time to
own that list!

Without thinking too much about it, jot down three things you
would like to experience sexually:

1. _____

2. _____

3. _____

Which of these can you mention to your partner? And how can
you most comfortably share your desires: by speaking, hinting,
gesturing, writing a note or a card, or texting? (You're not going
to want to use Facebook here, either.)

The Solution: Give Yourself Permission to Be Sexual in a Way That Works for You

Using your creative energies to do some fun problem solving
about caring for your sexual needs is energy well spent, and I think
your partner will agree. Think about ways you can make time for
sex in your and your partner's life, and then see how many ideas
you can come up with to make both you and your partner happy.

Allow Yourself to Have Sexual Fantasies

Part of the fun of sex is anticipating it, so allow yourself to do this. Here are a few fun and creative ways other women keep the fires burning. Can you think of others?

- Tuck a love note, perhaps with a hint about the evening to come, in your husband's briefcase or lunch.
- Send a suggestive text during the day.
- Call your husband and tell him in not-so-many words what you are thinking.
- Make a date for the weekend, complete with arranging for a babysitter for the kids.
- Surprise your boyfriend with some new undies.

Fight the "Too Tired at the End of the Day" Syndrome

Plan an afternoon lunch date with your boyfriend; creating a window of time in which you have more energy can be fun. You may even grow to enjoy sex in the daylight. Ask for some help with the evening routine. You may find yourself with some energy by the time the lights go out.

Don't Let the Kids Take All Your Energy

Go to bed when the kids do, forget the dishes and the laundry, and have some fun.

Bust the Boredom

Try something new: consider a good-morning surprise. Instead of faking an orgasm, move to a new position. And if you want some new stimulation, think sex toys.

When you stop listening to your girly thoughts telling you that you are not desirable and that you are not sexual or sexually exciting, you free up your creative energies to figure out how to take care of this challenge, which you haven't caused but which you *can* solve. Enjoy having your fire lit by owning your sexuality.

As you embrace your sensuality and sexuality, don't take personally the negative judgments you receive from others; remember, their girly thoughts are about them, not you. And be kind to yourself. I encourage you to get out—jump out, run out—of your comfort zone. It's not easy, but it will be worthwhile. Do something really nice for yourself today that encourages you to embrace the sexy woman you truly are.

DO'S & DON'TS

✓ Do have fun exploring what you would like sexually, even if only admitting it to yourself. Enjoy your sexual thoughts.

✓ Do something that you feel is racy: buy a book, a picture, some intimate garments.

✓ Do think sex toys; they are only toys.

✓ Do allow your sexual fantasies to occur throughout the day.

✗ Don't feel required to ask permission to have your sexual feelings.

Making Your Desire a Reality: Love, Intimate Relationships, and Marriage

> *To say "I love you" one must first*
> *be able to say the "I."*
>
> —Ayn Rand

> *Love yourself first and everything else*
> *falls into line. You really have to love yourself*
> *to get anything done in this world.*
>
> —Lucille Ball

> *How wrong is it for a woman to*
> *expect the man to build the world she wants*
> *rather than to create it herself?*
>
> —Anaïs Nin

Today's Detox Goal:
Create a Rewarding Intimate Relationship
That Works for *You*

From the time she was a little girl, all Yvonne wanted was to be married. "I'm in love with being in love," she said in one session with me. Unfortunately, this desperate need to be loved has led her to make some very poor relationship choices.

The Myth of Prince Charming

For many women, romantic love is the most important element in their lives. But in many ways love is the easy part. It brings us together, but does it keep us together? The answer is clearly no. Love is easy, but relationships are hard.

Enter the fantasy we've all been raised with: the intensity of our immediate romantic feelings will overcome all differences and allow us to live happily ever after. That promise is probably why the image of meeting "the one" is so enduring: it releases us of the responsibility of the difficult work of self-care. Prince Charming will be there to banish evil witches, take you to a wonderful world, and protect you. Even if you feel sure you've moved beyond this fantasy, answer these questions to see if it is still alive and well within you:

- Are you excessively focused on being married as the foundation of your self-worth?
- Are you a fan of bridal magazines and bridal TV shows, even if you aren't engaged?

- Do you secretly pine for someone who will be your partner and help you make decisions because you lack confidence in your ability to do this by yourself?
- Do you fantasize about the perfect wedding?
- Are you looking for an *instant* connection with a man that will let you know he's the one?
- Do you become angry with your husband or partner if he is not aware of what's in your head and is not making things right for you?
- Do you wonder if your husband is your soul mate?
- Are you married to the idea of getting married or staying married?

Girly Thought #5: Someone Loving Me Will Fill the Hole in Me

Yvonne is hardly alone in her quest for love. Of course love is important; it is a basic human need. But our girly thoughts tell us that we are incomplete if we are not adored and that this has to happen *today*. If your self-worth is tied up in being loved and being in a relationship, your girly thoughts are coming through loud and clear.

Ask yourself the following questions:

- Do you believe that your boyfriend completes you?
- Do you believe that love conquers all?
- Do you think of your husband as your "better half"?
- As a result, do you feel incomplete without someone who loves you?

Finding Mr. Right

I know you're reading this and saying, "She's wrong—my goal is to find *the one*." You believe that this is not only possible but necessary; furthermore, you think that if you have not yet found him, there must be something really wrong with you—that you are defective and basically unlovable.

Desiree felt this way. She moved from Los Angeles to New York City after college. As her friends partnered up while she remained single, she thought she must have some tragic flaw. "What is wrong with me?" she wrote on Facebook.

Let's look at how you go about finding your soul mate, the one who can't live without you. Do you do any of the following:

- Post a profile on a dating site that contains more than just a little exaggeration
- Join a gym even though you hate exercise
- Frequent hardware stores even though you don't need anything in them
- Hang out in bars even though you hate that scene
- Do speed dating and try really hard not to sound too smart in your five minutes with someone
- Go to meet-ups at baseball games even though you hate competitive sports, because these are better places to meet guys than in museums, which you like

If you ignore who you are and what you enjoy in order to meet someone who will unconditionally love you, how do you think Mr. Right will even recognize who you are? Does this make sense to you?

Settling for Mr. Wrong

As a result of having an unrealistic goal and blaming yourself for not achieving it, you might actually talk yourself into a relationship, ignoring what you do need and settling instead for what you can get, but secretly hoping you can change him. This is a tricky short-term proposition and a setup for a long-term unhappy and conflict-prone marriage.

Love Is Blind

Telling yourself you can put up with anything becomes the rationalization for not allowing yourself to know what you know. When you take off your blinders, what do you see? If your relationship is built on a fantasy of what you want the other person to be or hope he will become, you will not see the person in front of you.

It is not unusual to fall for someone's potential and then become disappointed when that person decides not to realize his abilities (Lee, 1989). Unlike the frog who turns into a prince with a kiss, your frog may be just a frog—perhaps a cute and totally lovable frog, but still just a frog. Maybe that's okay, or maybe it's not. Only you can know what's right for you.

Make a quick list of what you tell yourself is the perfect relationship:

_____

_____

_____

_____

_____

_____

Second-Guessing Instead of Talking

Assuming that true love means you will be able to communicate intuitively or telepathically can be a major stumbling block in a relationship. There are two common forms that this takes.

"If he loves me, he'll know what I want and need without me telling him." Relationships are built on many things, not the least of which is honest communication. But to be honest with someone else, you need to be honest with yourself and comfortable with stating what's on your mind (e.g., "I don't like the decision you just arbitrarily made") and asking for what you want (e.g., to stay in for the night or to try a different restaurant), even if you change your mind the next time the topic comes up.

"If I can just figure him out, everything will be fine." Women attempt to decipher the messages they receive from their male partners. "What did he mean by this? What is he thinking? What message is he sending?"

Are you really trying to understand the man in your life, or are your girly thoughts sending you on a treasure hunt? Are you really unclear and unable to communicate, or are you looking for clues that you are really and truly cared for, with the result that you blame yourself for the anxiety you feel about the relationship? And why have you made this relationship your job?

In couples counseling, I have witnessed so many arguments in which one party basically wanted the other to be in his or her head. It just doesn't work that way. Your partner is not a mind reader. Think about your relationship this way: if he is the one, you need to feel comfortable trusting him with your desires, your wants, and your needs. Doing this can be a win for both of you!

So many women see the man they want as strong and powerful yet treat him as very fragile, afraid that if they say what they need, he will run the other way. Let me be clear: if you want a relationship that works for you, you must be seen for who you are and loved anyway.

You need to *know* what you want and need if you're going to communicate those wants and needs. To achieve this, you need to have overcome the girly thoughts that tell you love has to look the way it does in songs, in movies, and in romance novels.

The Source: Fear of Honest Communication

Men and women communicate differently. Men tend to communicate though actions, not just words, which women do a fair amount of as well—we just tend to talk over our actions. Your girly thoughts insist that you have clear verbal communication from him, but are you as clear in return as you could be?

The fear of being alone is deeply ingrained in our culture. So is the fear that if you are an independent woman, you will be punished, as you will explore in Day 9. For many women, that punishment is abandonment, so they outsource the job of caring for themselves to someone else—someone who perhaps has all the answers. Research shows that women do this to be seen in a positive light, even when the price they pay is to also be seen as weak (Connelly and Heesacker, 2012).

This is a disaster, and you may have seen examples of it in your own family or with your friends. We all know someone who seems to lose herself when she's involved with someone. Nice girls win— or do they?

The Plan: Own What Works for You and What Doesn't

Your girly thoughts tell you that sacrifice is important, so you make what he likes to eat, spend time with his kids (even if you don't like them), fake an orgasm, and ignore your own wants and needs in so many ways that you begin to lose sight of who you are. I am not suggesting that you should never do any of these things to support the man you love. But ask yourself why you do them. Is it out of fear that you will be rejected? If you're going to confront your girly thoughts that tell you all men need to be catered to, that it's your job to keep your boyfriend or husband happy or else he'll find someone who will, then think again. According to research, feeling powerful can consciously help you in situations where you need to confront your fear (Van Loo and Rydell, 2013). So take advantage of the best that is in you: your resilience. Take a deep breath, speak on the exhalation, and say what you need.

Stay in Touch with Your Own Needs

In a good relationship, your partner wants you to be happy, and since we've established that partners aren't mind readers, you have to communicate what your needs are. But also know that focusing all your efforts on keeping your man happy is like building a house on sand. Happiness, just like every other emotion, is a fleeting experience. You can't always be at the height that happiness provides, nor can your partner. So putting so much energy into this part of a relationship can be rather counterproductive and create more of an illusion than a reality that all is well.

Speak Up

Learning a better communication style and putting it into practice may be difficult work, but are you allergic to hard work? Getting to know yourself, with all your quirks and contradictions, is
well worth it, so jump into you! Resist the impulse to tell yourself
that it's so much easier to rely on those girly thoughts to guide you.
You are worth the effort.

Realize When You Are in a Bad Relationship

You know that being in a bad relationship is expensive emotionally. Yet sometimes your girly thoughts tell you to stay in a
relationship even when another part of you knows that it is totally
not working. You feel torn, so you don't listen to the little voice
that asks, *What about me?* Instead you listen to your girly thoughts,
which speak to you about loyalty, not breaking up the family, how
much you are needed, and how love entails sacrifice.

If you are in a bad relationship—a relationship that is not supporting your needs, in which you cannot ask for what you need,
or in which you are being actively hurt in some way—you deserve
to address it. Despite what your girly thoughts tell you, when you
are in a painful relationship, you need to consider the following:

- Do you want this relationship to work?
- Does your partner want to make it work?
- Has this relationship served its purpose in your life and now
  it is time to leave?
- Can you have a *new* relationship with your current boyfriend
  or husband, this time not using girly thoughts as a guide?

This is not to say that at the first sign of any problem you should take a hike. Relationships of all kinds are complicated, and a love relationship is perhaps even more so because of all the added elements of love, dreams, sexual intimacy, and the promise of a long-term commitment.

Ending a relationship is sad, even when it's a bad one, but this also has its benefits. The end of a relationship means saying goodbye to the known, and that can be scary and painful. You grieve the end of unfulfilled dreams. But since they were *your* dreams, perhaps they can still come true elsewhere but look slightly different. Ending a bad relationship frees you up to begin a new one built on your knowledge of yourself and your understanding of what works for you to give and what doesn't.

Thus, it all comes back to you, but your girly thoughts keep making it about him. That's your inner tug-of-war. So many times I have asked women, "What is it that you want?" The thunderstruck, teary-eyed look I receive along with a shrug almost brings tears to my eyes as well. Rather than figuring out what they need and want, many women resort to doing all sorts of things that are clearly not in their own best interest, so they can "please" him, based on the notion, "If he's happy, I'm happy"—but it doesn't work that way.

The Solution: Free Your Inner Negotiator

Relationships require give-and-take, and this doesn't mean that you give and the other person takes; it means you need to finesse what you need. A bad relationship isn't just one in which your needs are not met; it's also one in which you can't ask for what you need.

But the million-dollar question is "What do I want and need?" I have found that women often want more connection with their partners. What they need is to spend more time taking care of themselves. For example, think about what you might ask from your boyfriend or husband so you will feel more connected. Could you do any of the following?

- Tell him you want him to ask about your day when he comes home.
- Ask him to call you at least once a day and see how you are.
- Ask him to bring home dinner so you can go to the gym after work.

Then ask yourself, *What can I do for me today?* These can be simple things, like picking up your dry cleaning (which has been ready for two weeks) or taking a few minutes to relax when you come home from work instead of immediately making dinner.

Does that feel overwhelming? Just think about this for today: What concrete actions can you take to get you closer to what you need or want? What is screaming in your brain and asking you to take care of it?

When you come out of the haze and confusion caused by your girly thoughts, you can begin to glimpse what makes a good relationship—one that involves loving yourself and finding someone who isn't afraid of you. That doesn't sound half bad, does it? It takes work, but don't get discouraged. Just look at how far you have come up to this point!

Girly Thought #6:
Being Married Proves I'm Lovable

We want so much to be loved and cherished that, for some of us, marriage becomes a goal that overrides everything else in our lives. Despite the divorce statistics, marriage still remains a dream for many women.

We are primed for marriage, but expecting the fairy-tale version of relationships is a surefire way to set yourself up for disaster. No relationship can make all of your hopes come true. Relationships are important, but they are not everything. The notion that marriage brings happiness and security forever is your girly thoughts talking.

The Source: Media and Family

Marriage is a destination for which women have been groomed (no pun intended) to arrive at full of dreams. To help us get there, we are raised with bridal Halloween costumes and Bridal Barbies. Think for a moment: are little boys prepped the same way? There are movies galore about getting married, more than there are about superheroes, and they all have the same plot: lonely girl seeks perfect guy to solve all her problems. To intensify this even further, the whole marriage industry is now the subject of several reality TV shows. The pressure to marry is very real, and it comes from all sides.

But in some ways the media just reflect family values. Families want their daughters settled, and to many, this still means married. The pressure may be indirect, as in "He seems like a nice man," or direct, as in, "Have you thought about children?" In her book *Marry Smart: Advice for Finding THE ONE,* author Susan Patton (2014) recommends that young women "relegate their hard work, in the classroom and the workplace, to the back seat and instead focus on catching a man in college, lest they risk becoming 'a spinster with cats.'" But do you really want to get married just to make everyone else happy?

The Plan: Determine What Is Best for You

This may feel like heresy, but when women consider the options, not every woman really wants to be married or be a mother. These are choices, and an increasing number of women are choosing to delay getting married or to stay single, with or without children. Here are some of the reasons a woman make these choices:

- She enjoys the life she has.
- She first wants to finish school, pay off her loans, and establish herself in her career.
- She doesn't want all the compromises she fears will come with this commitment.
- She's concerned her sex life will disappear.

You have choices. What is best for you? Ask yourself the following:

- Do you know yourself well enough to make a long-term commitment at this time?
- Do you fear having to abandon rewarding activities, friendships, and other relationships?
- Are there goals you want to complete before you contemplate changing your life?
- Do you fear losing your *self* in a long-term relationship?

Having a clear understanding of what you want and what you need is the first step in detoxing from the girly thoughts about intimate relationships. This is not selfishness—it is self-awareness. It is knowing yourself so you can plan what is best for you (Chirico, 2014).

The Solution: Self-Love

Women today are free to make many decisions that were inconceivable in previous times. But this puts pressure on you to determine what you need and not rely on having a partner or expecting the one you have to automatically know what you want and require. Perhaps this is why our girly thoughts are so appealing: they take the guesswork out of what is happening by telling you that something is your fault.

Instead of considering only your girly thoughts, instead of trying to be the good girl, consider loving yourself with all your desires and demands, even if you do not understand them. You know you can love others. You can forgive them for the times they hurt you, but can you forgive yourself? Can you love yourself, warts and all? Do you have enough confidence in yourself to make the best decision for yourself?

If you can love yourself, then loving another is possible. That's when marriage can make you happy: when you are a complete person joining with another complete person.

Keeping yourself in the picture in a love relationship is important. You are one-half of this relationship. It has to work for you, not just for him. Loving yourself, as well as loving the one you are with, can go a long way in making this a truly devoted relationship.

DO'S & DON'TS

✓ Do realize that you are a complete person; no one is your "better half."

✓ Do tell yourself "I love you" when you feel unloved by another.

✓ Do have fun not being the good girl.

✓ Do know that you have answers for what you need— you just have to listen for them.

✓ Do be kind to yourself. This is tough work. Do something really nice for yourself today.

✗ Don't believe there is only "the one" and his name is Prince Charming.

✗ Don't put someone else in control of your happiness.

✗ Don't be afraid to end a bad relationship.

Forever Youthful: Your Obsession with Staying Young

Nature gives you the face you have at twenty;
it is up to you to merit the face you have at fifty.

—Coco Chanel

Just 'cause there's snow on the roof doesn't
mean there's not a fire inside.

—Bonnie Hunt

I know people who are older than
I am who are twenty-five.

—Rita Moreno

Today's Detox Goal: Learn to Base
Your Self-Worth on Who You Are, Not on
How Young You Look, Sound, and Act.

Joy, age forty-two, shares the following: "Of course staying young is important. I still shop in that store Forever 21, I'm using Botox, and my voice still sounds young and kind of cute. And the problem with that is . . . ?"

Fifty Is the New Forty,
Forty Is the New Thirty . . .

Aging was once something your mother and your grandmother did. Not any more—aging is now a concern even for teens. Spas offer quince (for fifteen-year-olds) and sweet-sixteen Botox parties. In fact, at every age, Botox is now the most commonly used noninvasive surgical procedure (American Academy of Plastic Surgery, 2013).

This is a new world—or is it? Whether you are about to turn eighteen, twenty-one, thirty, or sixty, you carry an unnecessary burden about growing older. Guess why: those girly thoughts are everywhere, affecting how you see yourself and how you fear others see you, and they influence your actions, your decisions about money, how you dress, and even how you pitch your voice.

Girly Thought #7: I'm Getting Old,
and I Have to Do Something

Crazy, isn't it? "Aging means becoming unattractive" is a major girly thought for women. Even teens are told not to age. Whether you are celebrating your *quinceañera* or your sweet sixteen and are given your first Botox injection, or you're in your thirties and thinking you need a boob job now that you have had children, or you're in your fifties and considering your first face-lift, the need to appear younger has been thoroughly ingrained in you by our culture. Aging presents a major, almost universal, concern for women. You have been programmed to feel insecure about growing older since before puberty; you came by this girly thought honestly.

Think you're not affected? Answer these questions to see whether you are already having a problem with growing older:

- Do you think you can be desirable only if you are young and vulnerable?
- Do you worry about growing older even though that time is still far away?
- As you look at the older women in your family, are you afraid because there's no one you'd want to look like?
- When people speak about "the gifts of aging," do you wonder what the heck they are talking about?

The Source: We Live in a Youth-Obsessed Culture

Our society values youth and lacks reverence for our elders. In societies we have often labeled as "underdeveloped," the wisdom of those who are older is appreciated and sought out, even venerated. But this is no longer the case in Western society. Older citizens are now considered burdens. This translates into old age no longer looking like a comfortable destination, and thanks to your girly thoughts, you're ready to obsess about all the pitfalls long before you get there.

A commercial I find humorous is for a beer and shows a man (who is clearly in his sixties) skydiving, waterskiing, and then relaxing with several teenage-looking girls who gaze at him with looks of admiration. I laugh, but I also find it sad. As men age they are seen as powerful, but for women, getting old is thought to be not much better than a step above dying.

Many women believe the answer to inevitable yet unwelcome aging is to do whatever they can to turn back the hands of time. To that end, they pursue options that promise to restore the appearance of youth, including Botox and collagen injections, tummy tucks, liposuction, and face-lifts.

Author Rachael Stark (2014) wrote about just how commonplace this attitude is in an article for *Huffington Post* entitled "Why I Left a Botox Party":

> "Sneak away to a special girl's night out," the card read. "Join us for an evening of Botox and margaritas." I was surprised. I wasn't expecting an evening at my dermatologist's.
>
> A part of me was flattered . . . a gala for banishing wrinkles. But I was confused. Do I look like I need a Botox party? . . . I turned to my best friend, Mabel, for advice. Mabel has two kids, is [a] CEO . . . and runs a Girl Scout troop for tweens. [She said,] "Think of it as a modern Tupperware party . . . except . . . you're taking turns getting needles jabbed into your face—"
>
> "Ouch. Who'd want to spend Saturday night doing that?"
>
> Mabel shrugged. "Some people want to defy gravity."

Regaining Youth Through Plastic Surgery

Plastic surgery has become one of the first actions women take to change their appearance and attempt to regain their youthful looks; it is also the most expensive. But that hasn't stopped them from embracing it, and as a result, plastic surgery has become more socially acceptable and more desirable.

But many women choose plastic surgery out of fear. Kim had a face-lift and a tummy tuck after her divorce. "I was so afraid of getting out there and dating again. It's been almost twenty years since I've been single. I guess I felt that no one would be interested in someone who looks like me now." Now, you could argue that her surgery *did* give her confidence to date. But for the same amount of money, she could have gotten a new wardrobe and taken an exciting vacation adventure that would certainly be intriguing to discuss on a date. But no, she thought she needed something that made her look younger.

It is not just face-lifts that women are flocking to as antiaging remedies. There's also the buttocks lift, which does produce a cute and perky derriere to compliment your new perky nose; abdominal liposuction, which may be accompanied by the tummy tuck or else you're subject to sagging (and to go to all this effort and then sag just wouldn't be right); and the arm lift, which is becoming increasingly popular. I could go on, but I'm sure you understand that you can essentially fight aging in almost every part of your body through surgery. But do you really want to do this?

How Old Is That Photo?

A fairly widespread practice on social media and dating sites is to post a photo from a few years ago. But this is a short-term solution, and I've always wondered what happens when you meet someone in person who knows you only from that (sometimes decades-old) photo. Does he notice? Of course he does. This practice has the same downside of posting a selfie when you were fifteen pounds lighter—it promises a rather embarrassing first encounter. So why do it? Will it really make you any younger?

The Plan: Embrace Your Journey

Ask yourself whether it makes sense to fear your looks changing throughout your life. Does it make sense to try to look sixteen your whole life? It sounds silly, doesn't it?

So ask yourself whether you should spend your life afraid of the following:

- Pimples
- Wrinkles
- Gray hair
- Cellulite
- A deepening voice
- Stretch marks from childbirth
- A changing body shape

How to deal with this involves two decisions:

- Can you embrace inevitable change? You can learn to play with it by coloring your hair (a temporary measure at best, as hair grows), and being healthy. But consider the benefits of embracing the you of today instead of pining for the past.
- Do you want to spend your energy running from the inevitable: change? By wearing clothing that is more appropriate for your teenage daughter and spending a fortune on antiaging creams, you're falling for the promise the advertisers have been promoting. There is, after all, an entire business that promises youth, often for a hefty price tag.

The Solution: Realize That You're Doing This to Yourself

It is unfortunate that it often takes women a long time to realize that they are doing to themselves what others have done to them: denigrating themselves. But this doesn't have to be the case for you. You can change this, now, in your life by challenging the girly thoughts that say that once you age, your value diminishes. You're not a car that continues to depreciate as it ages. Do you want to continue being afraid that you're devaluing? If not, then don't act this way. Be proud of who you are and what you've accomplished, and strut your stuff.

With Age Comes Benefits

Think about some of the benefits of growing older and no longer being in the drama-filled years of your youth. Here's what you can look forward to:

- Your skin is clearer.
- You no longer have to be a slave to fashion.
- You're old enough to appreciate your parents and have your kids appreciate you.
- You know who you are and have less to prove.
- There's less you have to do and more time to do what you want to do.
- You can say good-bye to premenstrual syndrome.
- You can enjoy sex without the fear of pregnancy.
- You can relax; most of your major life decisions have already been made.
- You've learned many social skills and can be more engaged socially.
- You're happier and more able to enjoy the moment.
- There's more time to focus on your own health.

Make a note on those you've already experienced . . . and add some that are uniquely yours.

Girly Thought #8: I'll Seem Younger and Sexier if I Sound Like a Little Girl

Sexy baby voice, also called voice upping, is real. In fact, you or someone you know may be using it without having a term for it. Some "very smart women have taken on this affectation that evokes submission and sexual titillation to the male species. . . . This voice says 'I'm not that smart' and 'don't feel threatened' and 'don't worry, I don't want to take charge,' which is a problem . . . because it's telling women to take on this bimbo persona in order to please a man" (Monk, 2013).

Once you're aware of it, sexy baby voice, or voice upping, is rather fun to listen for. Here's how it goes: you make a statement, frequently at work, sound like a question by raising your voice at the end of the statement. Or you actually speak (in terms of pitch and tone) like a little girl.

Ask yourself if you raise your voice when you do any of the following:

- Speak to your boyfriend
- Want to sound sexy
- Find yourself in a tense situation
- Make statements at work

Your voice tells others a great deal about you. When you speak like a little girl in power situations such as at work, you are giving away your control. In an interview with Buzzfeed.com, actress Lake Bell had this to say about how we are judged as women:

> There are two main tells when you meet someone, and whether you like it or not, you're going to be judged by them. One is your visual appearance—what you're putting forth visually to someone. And the

second one is your voice, because that's your main form of communication . . . it's an opportunity to represent yourself. (Zakarin, 2013)

The Source: Society Values the Innocence of Young Girls

How we change our voice tells us, on an unconscious level, how we feel about ourselves, our desirability, and aging, defined here as reaching puberty.

Rather stunning, isn't it? Although speaking in a girly voice may make those who are past puberty feel more desirable, it has a downside, and here I'm not addressing how this may fit into the sexual fantasies of adults. Hearing this voice influences how young girls think it is acceptable to speak, reinforcing the message to avoid aging. Young girls try to increase or even maintain their naturally high-pitched voices, and this is raising alarms among parents and educators. Jessica Lahey (2014), a former English teacher who writes about education and parenting for *The Atlantic* and *The New York Times,* addressed her concerns this way:

> If women want to pass themselves off as pubescent in order to attract sexual attention, fine, that's their adult business. But when the trend spills over to *real* twelve-year-olds, who may or may not understand what the world hears and imagines behind that baby voice, I feel obligated to help them move toward a more mature means of communication that does not sacrifice content to its delivery.

Want to have some fun with this? Watch and *listen* to these short videos. You'll hear exactly what I'm addressing, and it is startling. Tina Fey took this on in *30 Rock* (*https://www.youtube.com/watch?v=uEmKN6DT-VE*), and in case you haven't seen Lake Bell's feature-length film, here is the trailer for *In a World*: *https://www. youtube.com/watch?v=NuxApRnekWc.*

In both videos, you will see and hear how the characters are coached to speak in a more *desirable* way. One video may indeed be worth a thousand words.

The Plan: Learn to Listen

Listen and notice how you and the women around you speak. This little change in awareness can tell you a great deal about yourself. Try not to laugh at your friends, but you may want them to know what you're doing. Many women don't realize that they are actually using sexy baby talk. Do the following:

- Listen for how you change your voice. Ask yourself if this is how you want to sound.
- Listen to your friends and mention to them what you hear.
- Listen to your daughter, her friends, or girls in your classroom or apartment building. Mention to them what you hear.
- Pay attention to the voice an actress uses in different scenes or in different roles. Ask yourself what she is trying to convey.

The Solution: Look Inward

Aging is not just about growing older. Listening to yourself is not just a reward for having gotten to the point in life when you have more time to direct toward getting to know yourself. Listening to your own inner wisdom can be extraordinarily helpful as you are growing and blossoming. Begin this today, no matter how young you are, so you'll have lots of practice drowning out the outside messages that tell you what is supposedly right for you.

Remember, as much as you are conditioned by your girly thoughts to find the answer to life's challenges outside yourself, the answers you need frequently lie within. But you have to learn to pay attention to them if you want to benefit from this true inner resource. So listen and learn from yourself!

Consciously Move Back into Your Life and Your Body

Right now, your girly thoughts are telling you to access outside things to "stay young," but that external focus will just continue to make you believe that there is something wrong with getting older. You need to tune out what is outside you that distracts you from listening to what is going on within.

Be the Healthiest Version of Yourself

Health is the real fountain of youth. A face-lift will remove excess skin from your neck, but it will do nothing to combat a lifetime of poor nutrition. Whenever you begin to be aware of what your body needs, whether at age fifteen or fifty, *aging* is really just another term for having the power and the responsibility for self-care. Here are some ideas to get you started:

- Educate yourself about nutrition and eat as healthily as possible.
- Move your body, not just to enjoy it but also to keep it strong.
- Meditate to relax and to remind you that within you is the power to change your mood.
- Make decisions based on your needs, not your girly thoughts.

Change How You Speak and Think About Yourself

Instead of focusing on negative qualities and telling yourself things like *I look so matronly* or *I can't let anyone know how old*

I really am, pay attention to how you've been feeding your girly thoughts, then switch things a bit. Try the following:

- Change your voice subtly in situations where you decide to make a specific statement. See what happens.
- If you decide to do some cosmetic things, have fun coloring your hair, getting a manicure, and getting a pedicure—but exercise to sculpt your body as well.
- If you are thinking of plastic surgery in any of its forms, think long and hard about why. Ask yourself whether this decision is based on loving yourself or on fearing life's inevitable shifts.

Decide How You Want to Value Yourself

You can continue to value yourself based on the norms of our society, but beginning in your teens you'll feel gradually more depressed as your girly thoughts become loud and clear and you lose this struggle. Or you can begin to define yourself and take control of your life, knowing you are who you are.

Mona e-mailed me, "My ninety-year-old mother-in-law is widowed and lives independently with a terrifically active social life. But when I visited her recently, she was nervous about an upcoming first date with someone new. I began to feel hopeful that just because we change on the outside doesn't mean we are any different on the inside. So perhaps aging is just what happens to our bodies, but not our spirits, where we remain in all our glory."

DO'S & DON'TS

✓ Do have fun playing with your appearance, but realize who you are and that your worth is what is inside; this hasn't changed since the day you were born.

✓ Do appreciate how you are changing as you are budding, developing, and growing.

✓ Do embrace the power you have to make subtle points just by the conscious changing of the tone of your voice.

✓ Do be aware of how younger women in your life hear you—literally and figuratively. Decide what message you are sending by your voice tone. Ask yourself whether this is the message you mean to send.

✗ Don't be held hostage by how others see you; take it as information about them.

✗ Don't spend your life worried about what *might* happen to you as you grow and mature. Enjoy your life by being healthy now.

Detox Summary for Part II

Imagine Your Intimate Life with Fewer Girly Thoughts

A body whose wisdom has never been honored does not easily trust.

—Marion Woodman

I always wanted to be somebody, but now I realize I should have been more specific.

—Lily Tomlin

You have just explored how you think and feel about yourself on a most intimate level. Doing this has demonstrated your courage and your determination to make real changes by stopping the self-sabotage of your girly thoughts.

List the self-defeating choices you have made about your looks, your sexuality, and your intimate relationship:

1. _____

2 _____

3. _____

Now it's time to change these. Let's keep it simple. Think about what you've just read and just tried.

- What excites you about changing your girly thoughts?
- List the specific belief you will target for challenge now.
- Specify new thinking about yourself that you will cultivate to replace this girly thought, even if it feels like a stretch.
- Consider how to gain support for doing this.
- Have fun listing the experimental actions you will take.
- Remember to notice your successes as you begin to detox from your girly thoughts, your negative habitual thinking about yourself. Jot down how you are making changes and share these with a trusted friend.
- Write new affirmations. Here are some examples:
  - ➤ I am perfectly imperfect.
  - ➤ I love my body, and my body loves me.
  - ➤ I am beautiful inside and out.
  - ➤ I know what I want.
  - ➤ My self-confidence is a powerful beauty potion.
  - ➤ My heart has practiced loving for a long time.
  - ➤ I love my real voice.

You can do this! Your hard work is worth it!

In Part III, you will look at how your girly thoughts specifically affect your daily life, inhibit your ability to be somebody, and derail your ability to function at your best.

PART III

Detoxing in Daily Life: How Your Girly Thoughts Affect You Visibly

Whatever you want in life,
other people are going to want it, too.
Believe in yourself enough to accept the idea
that you have an equal right to it.

—Diane Sawyer

Being a mom . . . I call it "lava in my spine."

—Jill Scott

Congratulations! You have completed the first two parts of your detox and are about to tackle the third and last part: how you see and treat yourself in the more public parts of your life. Here we shift our focus slightly from how you have been treating yourself personally to how you function in your daily life: how you are at work, how you handle your wealth, and how you are shaping the next generation, the legacy you are leaving your children.

Your girly thoughts permeate this part of your functioning as well, with the same toxic results. They cause you to shrink from your power, with pretty significant financial and emotional results. Remember to write what you discover in your journal so you can gain the confidence that has been lacking in your public functioning.

DAY 8

Starring at Work: Developing Confidence in Your Contributions

As women get more powerful, they get less likable.
I see women holding themselves back because of this,
but if we start talking about the success-likability
penalty women face, then we can
do something about it.

—Sheryl Sandberg

Don't be intimidated by what you don't know.
That can be your greatest strength and ensure that
you do things differently from everyone else.

—Sara Blakely, founder of Spanx and the
world's youngest female billionaire

Nothing will work unless you do.

—Maya Angelou

Today's Detox Goal:
Start Empowering Yourself at Work

We have so many girly thoughts about so many areas of our lives that it stands to reason they would join forces where we spend most of our adult time: at work. Is it any wonder that work becomes a place that can feel more like a minefield to be carefully maneuvered than a reward for all the dedication you've shown in going to school, working your way up the corporate ladder, and smiling when you'd really like to take someone's head off—especially when, as a result, you may still feel like you don't belong?

Camila worked so hard to have a seat at the table but kept feeling like an impostor. "All I did was doubt my abilities, feel they made a mistake in hiring me, even though they kept praising the turnaround in my division. The emotional cost of playing at this level took a great deal out of me."

Girly Thought #9: I Can't Get As
Far as a Guy at Work

The idea that you cannot be as successful as a man in your work environment is crazy. You certainly can, but you need to change your girly thoughts. If you hoped that putting in your time would pay off in fair and equitable treatment in your career of choice, think again. Work is anything but a level playing field. Men and women are viewed differently and treated differently, and the big secret is that we as women have something to do with this. Marie Wilson, a veteran of women's political movements, said, "When a man, imagining his future career, looks in a mirror, he sees a senator. A woman would never be so presumptuous. She needs a push to see that image" (Kay and Shipman, 2014).

Money factors in here, too. Instead of asking for the raises they think they deserve, women tend to accept what they are offered. This is particularly a concern for women early in their careers and can result in a substantial reduction in their lifetime earnings (Babcock and Laschever, 2003).

Wage Disparity Is Real

In an article in *The Atlantic*, journalists Kathy Kay and Claire Shipman (2014) address the evidence that women are less self-assured than men—and that to succeed, confidence matters as much as competence. Women at Hewlett-Packard applied for a promotion only when they determined that they were fully qualified. Men, however, tended to apply when they met 60 percent of the qualifications. "Underqualified and underprepared men don't think twice about leaning in. Overqualified and overprepared, too many women still hold back. Women feel confident only when they are perfect. Or practically perfect."

The pay disparity between the sexes has been constant for more than a decade, and it is the following:

- A constant in every state
- Worse for women of color
- A reality in almost every occupation
- Worse as a woman ages
- A problem even for women without children, debunking the myth that it is caused by women entering and leaving the workforce because of childbirth and child rearing (American Association of University Women, 2014).

The Source: Women Are Seen Differently at Work

We certainly see women in top management and in influential, elected positions. But to be accepted, women have to appear to be in control, to be steely in their resolve, whereas men in such positions are lauded for their occasional showing of emotions. Compare House Speaker John Boehner's tears at learning of a Republican victory to General Motors CEO Mary Barra's unemotional congressional testimony about the failure to recall 2.6 million defective vehicles.

This plays at all levels of almost every organization—men are praised for showing vulnerability, but women are seen as unreliable for theirs. Just think how women react when a male coworker wants to leave work early to make his daughter's game, the smiles he receives for being such a devoted and loving parent. Compare this to the last time you needed to leave work early for the same reason; were your coworkers impressed by your dedication, or did both men and women disapprove because you were letting your family issues interfere with your work? The expectations at work are definitely different for men and women.

When Elizabeth Morgan wrote her groundbreaking book *The Making of a Woman Surgeon* in 1980, she cautioned women that they could not settle for being as good as men but that they had to be better to be seen as equal. Since then, some things have changed, but others haven't. The challenge for a woman today is not to be better than a man; the challenge is to be her best, and this is where her girly thoughts keep tripping her up.

The Plan: Project the You at Work You Want Others to Know

Ask yourself the following to see whether you take your girly thoughts to work:

- Are you concerned about keeping everyone at work happy?
- Do you avoid confrontation?
- Are you concerned about doing everything perfectly so you won't be criticized?
- Do you try to get consensus on a plan? Are you reluctant to go ahead with it on your own?
- Do you keep generating new ideas even if old ones were shot down?
- Do you worry about failure?
- Do you feel like an impostor and fear you'll be found out?

Unfortunately, our higher standards prove to be more of a hindrance than a help, and they cause us to be too hard on ourselves; cautioning us to give up before we fail. Girly thoughts are expensive in the workplace.

The Solution: Allow the Professional in You to Make Decisions, No Matter How Uncomfortable That Might Be

There is a great deal we can do to influence the work culture if we challenge ourselves and stop setting ourselves up through our girly thoughts. This is not everything, but it can definitely make a difference.

I encourage you to stop your toxic inner dialogue at work and embrace your personal power. It won't be comfortable, and you might even need to *act as if,* to get yourself out of your current mindset, but this is how you invite yourself to grow. The key is that by now you know this is not as difficult as it sounds.

Girly Thought #10:
I Can't Do That—What if I Fail?

Many women learn early in life not to fail, and we carry this childhood fear into work. Women do well in school: statistics show increasing graduation rates for women at the graduate-school level. But work is not an extension of the classroom. Work performance is often on a group level, not an individual one. Rewards are given not for a fixed right answer but for flexibility and risk taking (Dweck, 2007).

Fear of failure is common for women. Unfortunately, over time, fear of failure becomes fear of risk, and that represents a very basic flaw in our thinking.

Failure is a great teacher: it helps you learn to walk, talk, read, do math, play soccer, and even how to date the right person. We learn through our struggles, through our ability to make things go as we wish, and through our efforts that don't go well at all. In *The Resilient Woman* I wrote about how we give our suffering meaning through the development of our resilience, the skills that come out of making sense of the things that we (and others) do that don't go as planned. Our resilience teaches us that our failures are a gold mine of experiences to be held, understood, and learned from because they point us toward the real answers.

The Source: Men and Women View Failure Differently

An interesting difference between women and men is how they approach challenge and failure. Men emotionally distance themselves from struggles at work by attributing failure to circumstances and their inability to control all the variables. Women often run from the same types of struggles; they wish them away, feel shame for having caused them, and use them as evidence that they shouldn't have gotten this job to begin with.

Why do men and women have such different viewpoints about challenge and failure? Kay and Shipman (2014) explain that in their youth, men develop confidence and learn to not take failure personally. They learn that they can get through a rough patch by attributing poor performance to poor effort, not to lack of ability. Their training grounds of sports and roughhousing, where they learned what didn't work through years of experience, are also strong influencers.

Men and women therefore arrive at work with different expectations for themselves. Men arrive with a set of skills that are better suited to feeling more confident in the work setting; for example, men are better able to compartmentalize problems in general and deal with issues separately. Women arrive at work ready to switch gears; they tend to feel their lives are in one big box, and everything in that box is competing for their attention. Women do focus on their work, but they do so with all their feelings and vulnerabilities, their to-do lists, their need to nurture relationships with their coworkers, and the desire to do their jobs perfectly. This creates a great deal of stress.

Women also tend to be burdened by taking full responsibility for everything. As a result, women hate failure because, unlike men, they take it personally. Failure is about *them*, about their lacking something, so it is something to be avoided because it is just too painful. Failure for women is not an object lesson to be looked at and be fascinated by. It is what they have learned to avoid experiencing, for it is further evidence that on some level they don't belong.

The bottom line is the difference between whether we attribute failure to an inner deficit or to circumstances (Dweck, 2007). That attribution leads men and women in very different directions at work.

The Plan: Don't Take Failure Personally

To determine if your girly thoughts are pushing you to do this more than you may have considered, ask yourself the following:

- Do your girly thoughts tell you to blame yourself for work failures?
- Do you think you should have known things you couldn't have known?
- Is it difficult for you to confront a coworker who has tried to sabotage you by giving you incomplete or inaccurate information?
- If something goes wrong, do you examine yourself to see how you personally contributed to this failure?
- Do you say "I'm sorry" even when you had nothing to do with what happened?
- Are you always trying to make things better for your coworkers?

The Solution: Free Yourself to Learn from Your Errors

As radical as this might feel, shrug off your mistakes and see what is to be gleaned from what didn't go as you thought it would— rather than being paralyzed, needing to blame someone else, or feeling ashamed. Ask yourself, *Hmm . . . what happened here? What does this situation tell me about what the next step should be? How can I approach this differently?* Treat your failures as a curiosity, not as a statement on your worthiness or competence.

Girly Thought #11:
I Need to Be Seen as Nice at Work

When you have a professional accomplishment, do you think you shouldn't say anything for fear you'd be bragging, and that wouldn't be nice? Do you attribute your professional successes to luck or to the rest of your team? This reluctance doesn't always translate well in the competitive environment of work, where results are what matters. Ask yourself how your needs to prove yourself and to be liked have played out in negotiating your salary or asking for a promotion.

The Source: Women Are Seen as Nurturers, Not Doers

Girls are taught to be nurturers. This is nothing new. In a paper written by a student at North Carolina State University (Starr, n.d.), the role of toys in pigeonholing girls was examined:

> Through popular toys such as "My Sweet Home" doll set, "Baby Born" doll, "My Little Helper Stove," "2-in-1 Vacuum Set," and the popular "Elegant Tea Set," young girls learn that their roles take place in the home. They learn that their duties require completion of household chores and nurturing the children. The descriptions on many of the packages tell the child the importance of their "roles." For example, the script on the box of [the] "Baby Newborn" doll set says, *Without you, Baby Newborn could not survive. Through your love and support Baby Newborn can grow to be just like you.* Messages like these tell girls that only they can provide a child with the love and care [the child] need[s] to survive, reinforcing the stereotype that women stay home and take care of the children.

Over time, this emphasis on nurturing diminishes our personal authority (Simmons, 2010). This is nothing new, either. In a recent study, girls shared that they felt pressured to take care of others, and nearly half said that they thought they shouldn't brag about what they did well. Their conclusions: act ladylike and don't cause problems (Girls Inc., 2006). Women who think like this never develop confidence in their abilities, and this sets up a vicious cycle that results in women being uncomfortable in starring roles.

As a result, your girly thoughts set you up to do the following:

- Blame yourself for what goes wrong
- Not take credit for what goes right
- Remain silent so you don't "rock the boat"
- Avoid demanding things that personally benefit you, such as a raise or a promotion
- Value relationships over everything else
- Be concerned about how everyone is feeling

Women Tend to Personalize Conflict

Your focus on being responsible for the well-being of those you work with has an unfortunate side effect: you spend so much time dwelling in the realm of the personal at work that you begin to see *everything* as personal, even routine disagreements. Whether the problem is with others or with the material women are dealing with, women tend to personalize their work conflicts (Nelson and Brown, 2012). Both types of problems are major issues for women at work because both drain and divert their energy from effectively solving the problems they confront, and instead their energy goes into blaming themselves.

Conflict at work is to be expected. Work is a place of almost constant negotiation of one type or another; resolving differences is commonplace. This is, after all, a group of people with whom you spend most of your time, and that presents ample opportunity for many levels of both understanding and misunderstanding to occur. Work provides a blend of numerous personalities with various skills who work together toward specified goals, all usually under some amount of pressure.

The Plan: Experiment with Being "Not as Nice"

See what happens when you are more direct with your coworkers. Don't automatically agree with them; your independent thoughts are important to your position, so freely offer your opinion. Yes, you may get the raised eyebrow and the look that means, "What got into you?" but you can enjoy an inner smile as you get on with your job. Note the results of this change of attitude in your journal.

The Solution: Don't Be Afraid of the Bitch Label

The flip side of being not so nice is fear of being called the dreaded word: Bitch. So accept that this is a risk you run if you allow yourself to be as brilliant as you are. You might shock some coworkers when you stop being so darned pleasant, so under-standing—so be it. Take off the kid gloves and let this be their problem. And you—well, just do your job using all the parts of you that resulted in you getting your position in the first place.

Showing your expertise and strength doesn't mean you have to suppress your caring side, though. If you have a disagreement with someone, invite that person for lunch or an after-work coffee to iron out issues and "bury the hatchet."

Girly Thought #12: The Women I Work with Are My Biggest Competition— or My Best Friends

Competitive feelings with other women at work often come out indirectly—you size up other women's looks, likeability, and work friendships. This proves to be expensive as these competi-tive feelings can cause you to feel mistrustful and wary of any women at work, which can potentially lead to your missing out on work allies. Similarly, those of you who feel that all women at work are trustworthy are also doing yourself a disservice. What's going on here?

Many women want their work relationships to be an extension of their families, and they see them as part of the loving, support-ive environment in which they will be cared for, in which their needs are treated as important, and in which they will be nurtured.

After all, we are not raised to be confrontational. But work has different rules, which is why it can feel like an alien place.

Work is not an extension of the personal realm, and this can be a rude awakening for women. The reality is that some women will hamper other women at work, whereas others will not. We see this in woman-to-woman bullying, which occurs from corporate to social service agencies (Brohl, 2013). "Many of us have witnessed the man who comments on a woman's hotness just as she leaves the room. But what about the woman who criticizes another's appearance (Did you see what she was wearing in there?) or frowns on a woman's unapologetic use of power (Just who does she think she is?)?" (Rezvani, 2012). In terms of actual bullying, women outrank men in under-the-radar acts (Lepore, 2014).

You're Coworkers, Not Friends

Fact: The men and women you work with are your coworkers, not your friends. Work is a competitive environment, and as jobs become fewer, it is important for women at all levels to understand that this is a different relationship from a friendship, with different rules and different expectations; it is also vastly unlike the competitive environment of the classroom, where women do well. This doesn't mean that you shouldn't have a friend at work; if you do find someone who can be trusted on the intimate level of a friend, that's great. But don't go to work to develop friendships. A major difference between men and women is that women often feel a need to bond at work, along with doing their job, whereas men are going at work to be recognized (Breslin, 2012).

Giving Away Your Power

The expectation of friendship results in women giving away their power at work. Anticipating that another woman will routinely help you or even become your buddy is a trap. When you let your guard down, you set yourself up for both personal and professional disappointment.

Psychologist Meredith Fuller (2013) discusses different personality types assumed by women at work that create problems for other women. Do you recognize any of these types?

- **The Excluder.** If there's nothing in it for her, you're toast. You're not seen, and information doesn't come your way, even if you need it.
- **The Insecure.** This is your micromanager who knows best, even if she's sorely lacking.
- **The Toxic.** This one drives you nuts. One minute you're her best friend, and the next she's stoking the rumor mill about you.
- **The Narcissist.** It really is all about her.
- **The Screamer.** This one could also be called the Drama Queen.
- **The Liar.** She is the mistress of all the shortcuts, excuses, fibs, and manipulations.
- **The Incompetent.** She knows so little that you actually feel sorry for her and keep helping her, but she does know enough to take the credit.
- **The Not-a-Bitch.** She is really just trying to get through and doesn't try to do more than this.

Take a moment and note which type catches you off guard or trips you up at work. Which type do you routinely find yourself sucked in by?

The Source: Women Are Taught to Enjoy Competition Less Than Men

Women act overtly less competitive than men. This is probably not biological; there are many examples in the animal kingdom in which the female is the hunter. But among humans, women have learned not to compete openly. This has been changing in the workplace, but it is proving to be a rough transition for women, especially with all those girly thoughts that tell you to be a good girl.

The Plan: Learn to Treat Your Coworkers as Coworkers

If you're not sure what it means to treat your coworkers as coworkers, you've just identified one of your major problems.

Many women continue to struggle with learning a new category of relationships in which they are required to develop different boundaries, have different expectations of those around them, and have the primary responsibility for taking care of themselves. This new category of relationships is called the world of work. To see where you are in learning about creating new boundaries, consider the following:

- Can you offer your solutions unapologetically?
- Can you be supportive of someone without being responsible for him or her?
- Can you challenge someone and not feel responsible for his or her feelings?
- Can you confront someone for the organizational good?
- Can you actively disagree with someone without feeling bad for him or her?

This is different, but different isn't bad. Different is just new, and new can be good. Work can be an exciting place where not only your expertise can grow but also you as a person. You are on your way to developing a mindset that will prove helpful, that doesn't include those girly thoughts, which only serve to decrease your effectiveness in a highly competitive environment.

The Solution: Be Responsible for Yourself at Work

You can't be effective at work while also being responsible for everyone else, even if it feels easier to take care of others than to be responsible for yourself. Directing others and holding them responsible (and being disliked for that, even if you are respected) is professional and necessary. It is not possible to be the office counselor, set limits on employees, and handle your area of expertise; let's face it, you have a great deal of experience in caring for others and less experience in sharing your ideas when they make others uncomfortable. You've been hired to do a job, so figure out how to do this and enjoy it.

DO'S & DON'TS

✓ Do understand that conflict is often a necessary and helpful tool in the workplace.

✓ Do be your own advocate.

✓ Do put your energy into learning the office skills to get ahead.

✓ Do take up more space at work and find ways to shine, such as the following:

> ➤ Send regular updates to your supervisor on where you are on specific projects so he or she will know you are working hard.

> ➤ Take public credit for your accomplishments.

> ➤ Speak up—offer your opinion in meetings.

> ➤ Be assertive. If someone states your point as his or her own, say, "Thank you for agreeing with this issue I addressed ten minutes ago."

✓ Do establish very good boundaries that allow you to disagree without blaming yourself for being disagreeable.

✓ Do learn to negotiate for salary increases and other benefits.

✓ Do develop your confidence by *directly* taking action. How can you develop confidence at work if you don't take action?

✓ Do remember that your coworkers are your competitors and your colleagues, not necessarily your friends.

✓ Do take care of yourself by being your own best friend.

✗ Don't try to be nice all the time.

✗ Don't be afraid of failure; be afraid of not learning from your failure.

✗ Don't take things personally. Conflict is normal and can be productive. Let go of the personal feelings you have about conflict and solve the work problem as you're getting paid to do.

Smart Money: Cashing In on How to Invest in Yourself

*We need to accept that we won't always
make the right decisions, that we'll screw up
royally sometimes—understanding that
failure is not the opposite of success,
it's part of success.*

—Arianna Huffington

*Money is the opposite of the weather.
Nobody talks about it, but everybody
does something about it.*

—Rebecca Johnson

*To fulfill a dream, to be allowed to sweat over
lonely labor, to be given a chance to create, is the meat
and potatoes of life. The money is the gravy.*

—Bette Davis

Today's Detox Goal: Remove the Emotional Component of Your Financial Decision Making

The topic of money is emotionally charged. Consider the amount of debt women carry on their credit cards; some of their spending is an attempt to compensate for how poorly they feel about themselves. Our beliefs about money cause relationship issues, strained friendships, and family fallout. Your girly thoughts have a field day with this area. But it doesn't have to be this way.

Renata came from no money and decided to change that. "As a teenager I put money aside from babysitting, even if it was just a little. When I had enough I began a very small online vintage clothing business. I watched my bottom line. I grew my investment in my inventory and myself. I figured it out, got professional assistance. Today, I'm a success."

As women we have so many insidious beliefs about money that hack away at our self-confidence; these attitudes have to be made conscious so we may tackle them as we have done with the other areas in our lives. Even when we are able to get past the girly thoughts that tell us we aren't good enough, many women still feel something holding them back: money. And I don't mean just the lack of it or the very real wage disparities women face at work. Our girly thoughts about money present a very real obstacle for us in believing in our own abilities, and they come out in some pretty stunning ways.

Money Is the Last Intimate Topic

You probably know more about your girlfriends' sex lives than you know about their salaries and bonus schedules. Clearly, we are more comfortable speaking about sex, even about how to have an orgasm, than we are about how much money we make and how we spend our money. This veil of secrecy about money produces many misunderstandings about how we can and should manage our own finances.

Girly Thought #13: I'm Not Financially Secure Without a Man

Women of past generations were taught that their goal was to find someone who had the resources to take care of them financially. This was part of how their girly thoughts told them they were loved. But today's woman doesn't feel this way, does she? When Celinda broke up with her wealthy boyfriend, she was disappointed by the lack of support she received when she told her friends, who are all professional women. Instead of offering her support and saying things like "Wow, that has to be tough," they reacted more along the lines of "Are you nuts? He's wealthy, and he treats you so well!"

Let's take a moment and examine your attitudes about financial security and your intimate relationships. Ask yourself the following:

- Are you more drawn to men who are wealthy?
- Do you believe it is your husband's job to be financially secure?
- Do you see your husband or partner as the provider?
- Does this mean he has to make more money than you do?
- Do you think you're just not good with numbers?

Answering yes to these may have been what women in past generations would consider normal and only fair, but do you, today, want to build your life around the need for a man to take care of you financially? Or do you have other requirements for what is most important to you in your primary relationship? If that is the case, then stop saying that money is number one when it isn't.

The Source: Women Still Don't Believe They Can Take Care of Themselves

As difficult as this may be to believe, in a recent survey, more than half of the women polled feared that they would end up destitute and homeless, even though they were making between $30,000 and $200,000 a year (Allianz, 2014). This stunning finding is attributed to the fact that although women have been making significant economic gains in the last few decades, they are afraid this can be reversed.

Women's "empowerment is tempered by the way women perceive themselves, as well as their beliefs about the impact financial independence has on others' opinions of them. Forty-two percent of the women surveyed by Allianz agree that monetarily independent women are less likely to find a romantic partner and more likely to intimidate both men and women. This fear of being undesirably independent was even higher among single women" (Gray, 2013).

How's that for some stunning girly thoughts?

The Plan: Take Control of Your Own Financial Future

Waiting for someone to come along and take care of you is a foolish financial plan. Whether you are in your twenties and just starting your career, in your forties and recently divorced and starting over financially, or in your sixties and fearing you'll never be able to retire, you must prepare for your own financial future. If you don't know how or where to begin, consider taking a financial-planning course (these are usually available through your local library or adult education), or consult a certified financial planner who can help you start down the right path toward financial security.

The Solution: Embrace the Belief That You Can Provide for Your Own Secure Financial Future

Achieving financial security is as simple as this: you must do it, and you *can* do it. If you're waiting for someone else to do this for you, you're listening to your girly thoughts, and by now you fully understand how undermining those are. You are a strong and capable woman; stop doubting your ability to handle this important aspect of your future and begin with baby steps—like opening a 401k at work—to provide for yourself. Knowledge is power, so educate yourself about money.

Girly Thought #14: I'm No Good with Numbers

This is an interesting thought: you're not good with numbers, so by extension you don't have the skills to manage your money. But is it true, or is this another example of your girly thoughts telling you you're incapable of figuring something out?

Emotional Decision Making with Your Money

When you allow this mantra to become your reality, you've set the stage for emotional decision making about your finances.

This belief contributes to women not making decisions that can help them financially and leads to the number-one reason couples argue: money (Heitler, 2013).

It is interesting that this is the last frontier for so many women who are educated, participating in the work force, and contributing to the family finances yet still uncomfortable managing their money.

Hannah always thought that making decisions about her retirement was beyond her, so she delayed it. When she began working for a company that offered a 401k, she didn't sign up for it. Like so many women, she decided she was still young and could use the money now; besides, she didn't really understand how it worked, and that made her anxious. "It's funny, I didn't put off getting an education. I didn't put off getting married, buying a condo, having a child. But this I felt was beyond me to figure out."

Hannah's anxiety about money did not exist only in terms of planning her retirement. "As I tackled this, I realized that I never spoke to my husband about our financial planning. This was somehow always his thing, and if I brought it up, we'd argue."

The Source: Money Has Traditionally Been the Purview of Men

Many women were raised with the idea that they were poor in math as girls. In previous generations, men were often the sole breadwinners, the only family members with the ability to make and have access to money.

This has been changing rapidly. The first women in your family to have access to money may have been your grandmother or your mother. So there are few role models. But is this enough to explain your thinking that this one thing is something you can't do? Financial advisor Suze Orman (2010) says it is something deeper.

We are now calling this "something" girly thoughts. The cultural belief that women aren't good with money has contributed to the development of your girly thoughts and has helped you to come to the conclusion that you do not have the skills to manage your money.

The Plan: Make Your Skills Conscious

You are a highly skilled woman. So of course you have skills you can and do use in more than one situation. Unfortunately, your girly thoughts have caused an odd gap between your skills and your ability to adapt them to manage your money.

Let's take a moment and list some of the routine things you do well that require a high level of skill that you perform without even thinking:

- Attending classes
- Running a car pool
- Managing your household
- Teaching a yoga class
- Managing your office
- Running a Girl Scout troop
- Singing in a local choir

You see, you are juggling several important areas in your life. Let's now look at the skills you effortlessly devote to these important but rather routine sectors of your life:

- Analyzing
- Delegating

- Investigating
- Organizing
- Supervising
- Creating
- Using your voice

The Solution: Recognize Your Skills and Make Them Work for You in Your Money Management

Anyone who can run a household or an office can manage her own money. It is just a question of using skills you've already developed and applying them in a new area. What stops you from making this transition is more about how you think about yourself than some fundamental deficit in your inner capacity—those girly thoughts again. Doesn't it sound strange to hear yourself say you can't manage another important area, from which you will personally reap the rewards from your efforts?

Challenge Your Own Thinking

If you don't need a man to help you understand finances, then stop acting as though you do. This attitude confuses your boyfriend, who probably sees you as a pretty independent person. It is costing you in self-respect and in your bottom line.

Augment Your Skills

Despite what your girly thoughts say, you do have two choices here:

1. Hire a financial planner with whom you feel comfortable working. Not only is there guidance available, but it is being made more

user-friendly for women who are conditioned to be uncomfortable with taking control of their money.

2. Go to school online or in a classroom. Become educated about the decisions you need to make to ensure your current and future financial well-being.

Voice Your Questions at Home

Money represents power and control in many relationships, so it is not an area in which to be subservient. Ignoring your financial situation is not going to make it better. Your girly thoughts may tell you not to make your husband or partner uncomfortable and not to threaten the relationship, but the cost of not speaking about money can be high both emotionally and financially. Whether you make more than he does and you don't want to make him feel uncomfortable, or you're a stay-at-home mom working with an allowance and consider his paycheck to be all his, you give away your financial security and your power in the relationship by avoiding these conversations. You deserve to know about your assets as a family because they represent some of your wealth, and you need to have a clear picture of your financial situation in case the relationship ends for any reason.

All couples have tensions about money. Don't let this be the dreaded issue that sits like a dense hole in your relationship and sucks up your energy. Bring this up and discuss it. Practice can make talking about money a little easier when you follow some clear strategies:

- **When you earn more money than your husband.** Many women feel uncomfortable when they earn more than their husbands do. Financial planner Faroosh Torabi (2014) suggests specific strategies, such as negotiating with your partner for his being responsible for specific areas within the family to balance out your making more money. We know money isn't everything, so we don't need to act as though it is. This can be an opportunity to value other contributions to your life together.

- **When you're uncomfortable discussing finances.** Share your discomfort. Is it about needing more money to keep the household going? Speaking about money will give him the opportunity to reassure you that he doesn't think it is all his and, if necessary, to renegotiate the amount of the household budget.

- **When you're a stay-at-home mom.** Your contribution to the family is priceless. But if you were paid, what would it look like? In 2014, the annual estimate of what you would earn if you were paid, based on the average stay-at-home mom's schedule of 94.7 hours of work a week, is $112,962 (Keeley, 2014). Proudly share your contributions with the family.

DO'S & DON'TS

✓ Do get out of your comfort zone about money. Learn to voice your questions and concerns.

✓ Do have fun planning your financial future—it is *your* future!

✓ Do explore your investment options; learn how to invest money for your retirement, how to manage an inheritance, or how to invest and protect funds from your first marriage.

✗ Don't think of money as dirty or something that you don't understand. It is a tool that is useful for you in living your life.

✗ Don't think that you are somehow less desirable if you are financially independent, but realize that you may be choosier in selecting a partner, and what's the problem with this?

✗ Don't think you need a man to help you make financial decisions. This is something you can figure out, and professional financial assistance is available to assist you.

Parenting: Tackling the Next Generation's Toxic Self-Talk

Women in particular are locked into being "little someone" to somebody else.

—Jane Pauley

Sometimes the strength of motherhood is greater than natural laws.

—Barbara Kingsolver

If it weren't for her setting me free, I might still be a caged bird today, holding my own daughter captive on a shit-laden perch.

—Rachel Cepeda

Today's Detox Goal: Avoid Passing Along Your Girly Thoughts to the Next Generation

Zara felt blessed that she had a daughter. "As a single mother, I vowed to not have her get caught up in all of the nonsense of being a women that I felt, my girly thoughts; and then she began school, and all my stuff came out in trying to protect her, which, of course, she felt she didn't need."

Like Mother, Like Daughter?

On Day 10, we've come full circle. You came to understand (on Day 3) how your girly thoughts were handed down to you by the women in your family. Now you are considering how to break this cycle. Girly thoughts are passed from generation to generation, and they teach the young women in your family to give away their personal power, to always wrap their self-worth in the embrace of this toxic inner dialogue.

You might not be able to prevent your daughter's exposure to the messages she receives from the outside, but you *do* have power over the messages you are sending. You teach your daughter—more often through example than through direct instruction—to speak, act, dress, and make sense of the world in such a way so that she is more appealing.

Think you're not passing along your girly thoughts? Think again:

- Does your daughter see you back off in family situations in which women are disparaged?

- Does your daughter hear you making nasty remarks about yourself as you look in the mirror? Does she reassure you that *she*
  loves you as she witnesses you not loving yourself?
- Does your daughter witness you trying to look or act young
  in ways that embarrass her, perhaps by your dress or your voice
  or by the pictures and posts you put on Facebook and other
  social media?
- Does your daughter hear you voice your self-doubts about work?

If you answered yes to any of these questions, then you need to
understand the power of your actions in teaching your daughter
your girly thoughts.

Girly Thought #15: It's Okay for My Daughter to Play at Being Sexy

Your daughter is exposed to subtle and obvious societal pressures. One is that she will be seen as a sexual object by the time
she reaches puberty, or even earlier (as young as eight). Remember
the term *jail bait*? This used to refer to girls in their teens; now
it refers to even younger girls, who often look and act older. It is
confusing to be seen as sexy when you're a kid; after all, what does
sexy mean to a nine-year-old?

I was confronted with this recently after a church service. A
woman I didn't know came up to me and asked to speak to me. She
shared that over the weekend her daughter had had a sleepover,
and one of the girls was wearing a necklace that said *sexy*. "What
does it mean?" she asked. Of course she knew what *sexy* means;
she just didn't know how to talk to her daughter and her friend
about what it means at age ten.

The Source: Our Media Are Highly Sexualized

Sexy is a term girls hear and use, but do they understand it? Part of our job is to help them understand this, because they will be assaulted by messages to be sexy. In our consumer-driven society where sex is used to sell virtually everything, these messages surround you and your daughter.

Young Girls Are Taught That Being Sexy Is Valuable

In many ways, sexuality is perhaps the most complex topic to discuss, because it taps into not just what your daughter may be experiencing but also what you might have experienced as a young girl. If you experienced sexual abuse as a child, this makes dealing with your daughter's emerging sexuality all the more complicated (O'Gorman and Diaz, 2013).

Your children, and you, are bombarded by sexual images. As a result they are particularly sensitive to the highly sexualized material in our media, which is present in the advertising of products, the characters in video games, even the characters portrayed during "family" TV shows. They lack the ability to fully understand the nuances, but they do receive a very clear message.

The power of being sexual is communicated very directly in the marketing of jeans, perfume, moisture cream, and even house paint, and it confers status, importance, and power. These are potent messages for kids. However, what our children experience through these messages about the importance of sex is that sex is sex for its own sake. It is devoid of any context of friendship, commitment, consequences, or romantic love. Kids conclude that buying the right products and looking acceptable—meaning sexy—is associated with being successful, having power, and commanding attention (Levine and Kilbourne, 2009). These become key elements of their girly thoughts.

Be a Consistent Role Model

It is often difficult to know how to direct your daughter toward healthy growth while also protecting her from these precarious sexual directives that she will internalize as girly thoughts. This often puts you in the role of being a strict parent, saying no to this or that, all in an attempt to keep your daughter safe. But all your daughter sees is that you are sending quite a different message to her than what you practice. "How come this is okay for you to post so you'll meet someone, but it's not for me?" Anna yelled at her mother about provocative photos.

The Problem with Looking and Acting Older Than She Is

One problem that men and adolescent boys have is that it is often difficult to tell the age of a girl who is acting, dressing, and speaking in a sexually provocative way. You may think she's cute. You may even think that when she's provocative in some way, *you* look more desirable—those girly thoughts do come in ways that are not desirable for either you or your daughter—but think again. Male attention can be confusing, even terrifying, for your daughter. On the one hand, this attention signals to a girl that she is an adult, which is her goal; on the other hand, she is not sure what to do with this—and that is not a good place for a girl to be.

Sexy Clothing

What happens when girly thoughts are put in charge of shopping? Sexy clothing! Young girls have always been slaves to fashion, as most mothers know. A colleague who is the principal of an elementary school told me he dreads warmer weather. "Bare midriffs, really short shirts, makeup—it's a nightmare to know what to do. Why do mothers buy this stuff?" he asked me in frustration. I smiled inwardly. He doesn't know how relentless young girls can be when shopping. He has a boy.

Sexy Baby Voice

We discussed voice on Day 7, but it bears repeating here specifically for your daughter. Although you may think that talking in a little girl's voice makes you cute and desirable, it can have totally undesirable consequences for her. Ask yourself, is this how you want your daughter to speak? If not, then you need to address this directly.

The Plan: Help Your Daughter Grow Safely into Her Sexuality

Your daughter needs strategies for dealing with the girly thought challenges she will encounter while growing up. These strategies will give her confidence. As her mother, you can help her learn to do the following:

- Ask questions of you and other adults.
- Confront unwanted looks and comments by saying, "You're disgusting—I'm only eleven!"
- Dress in a way that sends the message she intends.
- Act and sound her age.
- Resist peer pressure to go along with the crowd and be sexualized.

Ask your daughter about her emerging girly thoughts:
- The pressure she feels to look and act a certain way

- Her desire to be an adult and sure of herself instead of being in this in-between place
- Her fear that she may be rejected if she does something different

I recently had a young woman share with me why she cut off her long hair. "It's like this girly thought thing in my school for all the girls to have this long sexy hair," she said, "and I thought, it's not me. So I cut my hair, myself, short. I look in the mirror now and I see myself, not who someone decided I'm supposed to be."

The Solution: Speak Early and Often about Sexuality and Girly Thoughts

Give your daughter the name for her toxic, inner dialogue. Talk to other family members and friends about sharing their own girly thoughts with your daughter. Talk with her about shows and ads on TV and in her favorite magazine. Watch some movies together and discuss the girly thoughts there. A good movie to start with might be *Mean Girls*:

- Ask her what Regina and Cady are trying to convey.
- Discuss how Regina and the rest of the Plastics see Cady. How do Janis and Damian see her?
- How desperate do you think Cady is to be accepted?
- What would happen if she were just herself?
- What price is she paying by going along with her girly thoughts?

The more you speak to your daughter about girly thoughts, the easier it will be for you to discuss and for her to hear.

Understand Your Own Feelings about Sexuality

We addressed this on Day 5, but it bears looking at again, this time through the eyes of your daughter. What messages did you receive when you were growing up? Obviously, your early history and experiences have tremendous power to shape you and for you to shape your daughter. Consider the following:

- What were your parents' attitudes toward sexuality that were problematic for you and that helped you form your girly thoughts? How might you be carrying these forward?
- If there was sexual abuse in your family and this helped to form your girly thoughts about what you needed to do and not to do to be loved, how can you now take care of yourself? How can you address the understandable fears you may have for your daughter? It is important to determine how to care for yourself so that your daughter doesn't begin to think that she has to care for you instead of herself, which would produce another generation of codependency.
- What messages did you receive from your religious leaders that contributed to your girly thoughts? Is your daughter receiving similar messages? What can you do to support her?

Listen to How She Speaks

If your daughter is using sexy baby voice, first monitor your own voice. Are you falling into using a sexy baby voice that your girly thoughts say is important? If your daughter views you as her role model, she'll imitate a great many of your actions. Remind her to use her "big girl" voice.

Girly Thought #16: I Feel I Should Be My Daughter's Best Friend, But I Don't Have any Influence Over Her

You don't need to be your daughter's best friend—you need to be her mother. You need to help your daughter with her girly thoughts, and not all of what you have to do will make her see you as a peer. As a friend you probably don't have much influence, but as a mother, you have it through the following:

- Your own actions
- The controls you set up
- The conversations you have with your daughter, as uncomfortable as they might be

Young girls are greatly influenced by their friends and the media telling them that they need to do certain things to become and remain popular. Remember when popularity was so important? But the ways girls are popular now, the signs of being accepted, are very different from what they were when you were a girl that age.

Maybe being popular is too important to her. Following specific conventions to gain and/or keep her popularity is another indication that she is ruled by her own girly thoughts.

The Source: Your Daughter Is the New Marketing Target

The media-saturated world your children are being reared in produces some of the same stresses you experienced, but on a much more intense level. As a result, not only is your daughter having girly thoughts, she is also being constantly buffeted by messages that reinforce them.

You can't prevent girly thoughts from entering your daughter's life altogether. You can't (and shouldn't) seal your child in a protective bubble, no matter how appealing this might seem. But what you *can* do is poke your finger in the eye of her developing girly thoughts and prevent them from taking hold.

Whatever pressures you may have felt to be popular, to have the latest thingamajig, have been magnified by the advent of our current intense media in all their forms. There is so much media attention on young girls because it translates into a new revenue stream, and a very lucrative one at that.

Dress and Gadgets

Tweens—children ages eight to twelve (Hotta, 2014)—represent the newest marketing group, a "golden egg" worth an estimated $43 billion in 2011 (Wells, 2011). Slick marketing convinces them to demand from their parents the best their parents' money can buy. This is a group with highly disposable income, even if it is just their allowance, and with parents who are often busy and distracted just trying to make the family life work. Do you feel the pressure? The manufacturers surely hope so. One mom told me she went shopping with her daughter for jeans. "But once we were in the mall, I ended up buying her a tablet. I couldn't stand any more arguing."

Do You Focus on Youth?

Your daughter watches you carefully, looking for clues for what she can expect when she reaches the magical threshold of adulthood. Although what you say is important, it's less so than what you do. Your daughter learned to nurture her dolls by imitating you; observing what upsets you and the conclusions you draw from what is around you influences her. Whether you're fretting about gaining weight, going gray, or thinking you need plastic surgery to look younger, your daughter is watching and making sense of what she sees you doing and saying.

The Plan: Focus Your Daughter on Healthier, More Sustainable Ways to Feel Good About Herself

Let's construct a solid plan. You know your daughter better than anyone else does.

Help Her Be Aware of Digitally Altered Images

Have fun together searching for digitally altered images. See which ones she thinks have gone too far. Introduce your daughter to Sexualization Protest: Action, Resistance, Knowledge, or SPARK (*www.sparksummit.com*), a girl-driven movement that works directly with girls and young women ages thirteen to twenty-two to train them to be media activists and leaders in the fight against the sexualization of girls in the media. Maybe she'll become an activist.

Teach Her About the Power of Her Money

Hold the line on purchases. Help her understand how her finances have to be balanced. Assist her in earning money and learning to manage it. Teach her to save for what she would like to own.

Monitor Facebook and Other Social Media

Ask to be your daughter's Facebook friend. Monitor her posts. Speak to her about social media, even though she won't want to do so. Tell her to take down suggestive photos or posts. She'll scream, but she'll probably listen, and you've just given her the best cover: "My mother made me do it!"

Facilitate Her Sense of Belonging

Work with your daughter to help her develop places she can belong, such as the following:

- In school: after-school clubs, in-school events, science projects, musicals, and sports. Push your school to develop these, with parents volunteering their specific expertise.
- In the community: ballet, church choir, horseback riding, 4-H Club, or Girl Scouts. There are many opportunities for face-to-face contact, and they all should be understood and explored to see what the best matches will be for your daughter. In your busy life, you can do this by partnering with other parents to get ideas and share transportation.

Help Her Be Her Best

It is natural for girls to want to excel, but it is not so easy to find an area in which they can do so. Parents sense this and try to fill this need by endlessly praising their daughters, but praise does not necessarily guide them in figuring out what their best can be. How can you help your daughter with this? Try the following:

- Help her understand when her girly thoughts get in the way of her being the person you know her to be. We can't change something until we know it's a problem for us.
- Notice and congratulate her achievements: give her a card after reading her poetry, buy her flowers after a concert, or take her out for ice cream after a soccer game. Let her know you see her, even if she acts like this is a bore.

- Understand her very real challenges and support her in these, whether she's giving an oral report or handing in an art project. Confronting her own anxieties is a cause for celebration.
- Create ways for her to shine. Perhaps this is learning to bake a cake, training the family dog, or even volunteering at a community event. Mastery can and should take many forms.

Help Her Make Peace with Her Body

Share what you learned about your own girly thoughts about beauty on Day 4, and encourage her to focus on her strength and her agility, not on her chunkiness or her height. Once a girl hits puberty, her body changes so fast that it can feel like it doesn't belong to her anymore. Help your daughter develop strategies to deal with suddenly having a woman's body, and remind her that the solution to many body anxieties is a healthy lifestyle: exercise, nourishing food, and adequate rest.

Help Her Deal with Her Emerging Sexuality

Remember when you were first addressing this in your own life. How were your emerging sexual feelings influenced by your girly thoughts? This might give you some insight that can help you guide your daughter to understand that her sexuality is an exciting part of herself that she needs to keep safe and not use to garner even more attention.

Say No in a Complete Sentence

Part of being a parent is learning to set clear boundaries, even if your girly thoughts say otherwise. There will probably be a meltdown, and it won't be the first or the last. Part of being a parent is learning to weather this.

Show Her That She Has Choices

This is an opportunity to use what you have learned and begin to send a different message to your daughter. Let her know what you have been working on—your girly thoughts and what you have discovered: that looks are not everything, that what you want might not be popular, and that you have a right to make choices that work for you. Help her see how making the choices that are right for her will make her happier than if she tries to follow the crowd.

The Solution: You Need and Deserve Support

As a parent, you have less and less control as your daughter grows up, but you still have influence. The major area of influence you have is in how you allow your girly thoughts to craft the life you lead, for this is what she will feel, hear, and see.

Your Daughter Is a Child of the "Village"

Parenting was never meant to be the sole responsibility of one person who is able to do this only part-time. You need and deserve lots of support to address how to deal with your daughter's girly thoughts, so share what you have learned about the importance of having the term *girly thoughts* to capture this range of self-doubt. Consider the following:

- Speak to her father about your concerns. Even if her father is no longer living with the family, he is an important influence on your daughter and her girly thoughts.
- Address the seduction of girly thoughts at PTA meetings, in parenting groups at your house of worship, and with other influential adults who come in contact with your daughter and other girls.

- Speak to her Girl Scout leader about girly thoughts.
- Discuss girly thoughts with your friends and the mothers of your daughter's friends.
- Address girly thoughts with the rest of family, particularly those who also have daughters.
- Consider consulting with a mental health professional, if necessary.

Use Available Resources

Fortunately, there are numerous resources for parents. Become an educated consumer and see which ones of the following are best for you:

- Articles in magazines and on blogs that address your concerns and support your viewpoint
- Books
- Talks sponsored by medical or educational organizations
- Parenting support groups
- Online chat groups

Consider Your Own Part in Feeding Her Girly Thoughts

You've just spent ten days considering the ways your girly thoughts have affected you in major sectors of your life. Go through each day and list how each of your own girly thoughts might be affecting your daughter in these areas of her life.

DO'S & DON'TS

✓ Do watch out for when you are inadvertently sending the message "Do as I say, not as I do." Your daughter, your granddaughter, and your nieces will learn more from what you do than what you say. So do it well.

✓ Do become aware of your own girly thoughts. Remember that you are your daughter's role model for all things female.

✓ Do live a healthy lifestyle that includes healthy eating and physical activity as priorities.

✓ Do help her pick out clothing that is age-appropriate.

✓ Do point out digitally altered images in the media.

✓ Do help her watch for girly thoughts in Facebook posts.

✓ Do have fun watching TV shows and movies and reading magazine articles and books to look for and point out the girly thoughts of the characters.

✓ Do talk to her about the relationship choices you see her making. Encourage her not to take full responsibility for any relationship.

✗ Don't give her a nose job, breast implants, or a Botox injection as a birthday or holiday gift. These all reinforce the idea that her body needs to be fixed to make her more desirable.

✗ Don't obsess about your weight in front of your daughter, because this will teach her to focus on her own weight as a way of judging her self-worth.

✗ Don't fret over aging and being unattractive. This may cause her to feel the need to take care of you, setting her up for a possible next generation of codependency. It also reinforces the idea that eternal youth is a desirable goal.

Keep in mind that the changes you make will affect not only your daughter but also your daughter's daughter.

Detox Summary for Part III

Seeing Your Daily Life Free of Girly Thoughts

Think like a queen.
A queen is not afraid to fail.
Failure is another stepping-stone to greatness.

—Oprah Winfrey

There came a time when the risk to
remain tight in the bud was more painful
than the risk it took to blossom.

—Anaïs Nin

You have just tackled some of the thorniest problems women face: work, money, and how we fear we are treating our children.

List the messages your self-defeating girly thoughts have given you about yourself, your work, how you manage your money, and how you parent your children:

1. _____

2. _____

3. _____

Now it's time to change these. Let's keep it simple. Think about what you've just read and just tried and answer the following:

- What excites you about changing your girly thoughts?
- List the specific belief you will target for challenge now.
- Specify new thinking about yourself that you will cultivate to replace this girly thought, even if it feels like a stretch.
- Consider how to gain support for doing this.
- Have fun listing the experimental actions you will take.
- Think how you would like to affirm yourself, when you're thinking a girly thought, that will help you move past the thought. Here are some additional affirmations:
  - ➤ I can bring my whole self to you. I am your mother.
  - ➤ I will stop perpetuating the scripting of girly thoughts in the next generation.
  - ➤ I can and will ask for what I deserve.
  - ➤ I will negotiate, not acquiesce.
  - ➤ I will enjoy the power of my money.
  - ➤ The most important thing I wear is my confidence.

Remember to notice your successes as you begin to detox from your girly thoughts, your negative habitual thinking about yourself. Jot down how you are making changes, and share these with a trusted friend.

Enjoy pushing past your girly thoughts and reveling in the real you that was obscured: beautiful, powerful, focused, and fun.

Just the Beginning: Now the Fun Starts

Follow your passion. Stay true to yourself.
Never follow someone else's path unless you're in
the woods and you're lost and you see a path.
By all means, you should follow that.

—Ellen DeGeneres

I hope you have found *The Girly Thoughts 10-Day Detox Program* a helpful path in directing you to be true to yourself.

By now you realize that you are not crazy. Beliefs have been handed down from mother to daughter, taught in your family stories, internalized in your own life script, hammered into you by society, and affecting all domains of your life—from how you feel about sex and your body to how you parent to how you function at work and manage your money. These may have shaped your life to this point, but they don't have to any longer.

You now have a term to describe this inner phenomenon, which has been pinpointed by various authors as a cause of concern (Orman, 2010), as the reason that women are afraid and "silence themselves" (Sandberg, 2013), as the reason that women lack confidence (Kay and Shipman, 2014), and as the reason that even women who make $200,000 a year fear that they could become bag ladies (Allianz, 2014). That term is *girly thoughts*. Use it.

You now also realize that you are not alone. In your office, in your family, in your apartment building, on the street, and in the media, women have girly thoughts. It is fascinating that once you understand this inner sabotage, you can see it everywhere.

You understand that girly thoughts are far from benign. They form an inner toxic soup that prompts self-defeating choices. You have examined your own girly thoughts, identified the choices influenced by them, committed yourself to challenge these thoughts, and have even begun to appreciate the new you who is no longer burdened by negative self-talk. As a result, you're unapologetically enjoying your own personal power.

Whew! But the process is not over; it's actually just beginning. You need to stay aware of your thinking. If you get too comfortable, you will begin to backslide, because the cues that keep your girly thoughts going are all around you. You need to keep challenging those self-defeating thoughts when they attack you and remind you to be the good girl, don't make waves, and so on.

> Only you can make this change within yourself, but you don't have to do it alone.

There is a great deal of support available to you in challenging your girly thoughts, and you are worth the time and effort it takes to access any or all of these as you step into your personal power. After all, those girly thoughts are well entrenched.

One way to keep your focus on changing your girly thoughts is to share what you have learned with those you are close to: your friends and your family. Help expose the girly thoughts of the women in your life.

Remember: Behind every successful woman is a best friend giving her "crazy ideas."

References and Recommended Reading

Allianz. 2014. "Women, Money, and Power." May 5. https://www.allianzlife.com/retirement/retirement-insights/women-money-and-power 5.5.14

American Academy of Plastic Surgery. 2013. "14 Million Cosmetic Plastic Surgery Procedures Performed in 2012." http://www.plasticsurgery.org/news/past-press-releases-archives/2013/14-million-cosmetic-plastic-surgery-procedures-performed-in-2012.html

American Association of University Women. 2014. "The Simple Truth About the Gender Pay Gap." March 10. http://www.aauw.org/research/the-simple-truth-about-the-gender-pay-gap/ 3.10.14

Amoruso, S. 2014. *#Girlboss*. New York: Portfolio.

Babcock, L., and S. Laschever. 2003. *Women Don't Ask: Negotiation and the Gender Divide*. Princeton, NJ: Princeton University Press.

Bem, S. L., and D. J. Bem. 1970. "Case Study of a Nonconscious Ideology: Training the Woman to Know Her Place." In *Beliefs, Attitudes, and Human Affairs*, edited by D. J. Bem, 89–99. Belmont, CA: Brooks/Cole.

Bergner, D. 2013. *What Do Women Want? Adventures in the Science of Female Desire*. New York: Ecco.

Black, H. 2009. *The Secret Currency of Love: The Unabashed Truth About Women, Money, and Relationships*. New York: William Morrow.

Breslin, S. 2012. "Three Ways Women Undermine Themselves at Work." May 22, 2012. http://www.forbes.com/sites/susannahbreslin/2012/05/22/women-undermine-themselves-at-work/

Brohl, K. 2013. *Social Service Workplace Bullying: A Betrayal of Good Intentions*. Chicago, Illinois: Lyceum.

Butler, B. "Lupita Nyong'o's speech on 'black beauty' underscores her significance in Hollywood." March 01, 2014. http://www.washingtonpost.com/blogs/she-the-people/wp/2014/03/01/lupita-nyongos-speech-on-black-beauty-underscores-her-significance-in-hollywood/

Chirico, K. "The 15 Best Parts of Being Single in Your Thirties." January 4, 2014. http://www.buzzfeed.com/kristinchirico/the-15-best-parts-of-being-single-in-your-thirties.

Connelly, K., and M. Heesacker. 2012. "Why Is Benevolent Sexism Appealing? Associations with System Justification and Life Satisfaction." *Psychology of Women Quarterly* 36 (4): 432–43.

Cox, D. "Female Action Heroes." December 12, 2013. http://www.theguardian.com/film/filmblog/2013/dec/12/female-action-heroes-katniss-role-models-women

Dockterman, Eliana. "And the New Wonder Woman Is . . ." December 4, 2013. http://entertainment.time.com/2013/12/04/and-the-new-wonder-woman-is/

Dweck, C. 2007. *Mindset: The New Psychology of Success—How We Can Learn to Fulfill Our Potential.* New York: Random House.

Ellwood-Clayton, B. S. 2013. *Sex Drive: In Pursuit of Female Desire.* Crows Nest, Australia: Allen & Unwin.

Estés, C. P. 1996. *Women Who Run with the Wolves: Myths and Stories of the Wild Woman Archetype.* New York: Ballantine Books.

Fields, H. 2012. "What Is So Good About Growing Old?" *Smithsonian*, July. http://www.smithsonianmag.com/science-nature/what-is-so-good-about-growing-old-130839848/?no-ist, July 2012.

Fuller, M. 2013. *Working with Bitches: Identify the Eight Types of Office Mean Girls and Rise Above Workplace Nastiness.* Cambridge, MA: Da Capo Lifelong Books.

Girls Inc. 2006. *The Supergirl Dilemma: Girls Grapple with the Mounting Pressure of Expectations.* New York: Girls, Incorporated.

Gray, E. 2013. "Women Fear Becoming 'Bag Ladies.'" *Huffington Post*, March 28. http://www.huffingtonpost.com/2013/03/27/women-fear-becoming-bag-ladies-study_n_2967675.html

Heffernan, L. 2014. "Princeton Mom Gives Dumb Advice on Marrying Smart." *Forbes*, March 11. http://www.forbes.com/sites/deborahljacobs/2014/03/11/princeton-mom-gives-dumb-advice-on-marrying-smart/

Heitler, S. 2013. "Fighting About Money—Beware!" *Psychology Today*, September 17. http://www.psychologytoday.com/blog/resolution-not-conflict/201309/fighting-about-money-beware 9.17.13

Hotta, Lisa Tabachnick. "Care Stages: How Does My 'Tween Grow? Ages 8 to 12." Care.com, July 22, 2014. http://www.care.com/a-care-stages-how-does-my-tween-grow-ages-8-1201251204

Jong, E. 1973. *Fear of Flying*. New York: Signet Books.

Jost, J. T., and A. C. Kay. 2005. "Exposure to Benevolent Sexism and Complementary Gender Stereotypes: Consequences for Specific and Diffuse Forms of System Justification." *Journal of Personality and Social Psychology* 88:498–509.

Kaplan, E. 2012. "Women and Money: Why They Avoid Risk and Lack Confidence When Making Decisions." *Forbes*, November 20. http://www.forbes.com/sites/feeonlyplanner/2012/11/20/women-and-money-why-they-avoid-risk-and-lack-confidence-when-making-decisions/

Kay, K., and C. Shipman. 2014. *The Confidence Code: The Science and Art of Self-Assurance—What Women Should Know*. New York: Harper Business.

Keeley, H. 2014. "The Real Salary of a Stay-at-Home Mom." http://hannahhelpme.com/blog/the-real-salary-of-a-stay-at-home-mom 2014

Kilbourne, J. 2000. *Can't Buy My Love: How Advertising Changes the Way We Think and Feel*. New York: Free Press.

Lahey, J. 2014. "Why Middle-School Girls Sometimes Talk Like Babies." *Atlantic*, February. http://www.theatlantic.com/education/archive/2014/02/why-middle-school-girls-sometimes-talk-like-babies/283894/

Lee, J. 1989. *The Flying Boy: Healing the Wounded Man*. Deerfield Beach, FL: Health Communications, Inc.

Lepore, M. "Happy 50th Birthday Michelle Obama! Here Are 6 of Her Best Quotes." January 17, 2014 http://www.levo.com/articles/lifestyle/michelle-obama-best-quotes

———. "Mean Girls at Work: Why Women Are Bullies." February 10, 2014. http://www.levo.com/articles/career-advice/mean-girls-at-work.

Levine, D., and J. Kilbourne. 2009. *So Sexy So Soon: The New Sexualized Childhood and What Parents Can Do to Protect Their Kids*. New York: Ballantine Books.

Martin, C. E. 2007. *Perfect Girls, Starving Daughters: The Frightening New Normalcy of Hating Your Body*. New York: Free Press.

Merzenich, M. 2013. *Soft-Wired: How the New Science of Brain Plasticity Can Change Your Life*. San Francisco: Parnassus.

Monk, K. "Interview 'In a World'—Film Director Lake Bell with Video." August 14, 2013. http://o.canada.com/entertainment/movies/0815-film-world-bell.

Morgan, E. 1980. *The Making of a Woman Surgeon*. New York: Putnam.

Morrigan, C. 2013. http: thoughtcatalog.com/Charlie-Morrigan/2013/04/the-69-greatest-quotes-about-sex.

Nelson, A., and C. Brown, C. 2012. *The Gender Communication Handbook: Conquering Conversational Collisions Between Men and Women*. New York: Pfeiffer.

O'Gorman, P. 2013. *The Resilient Woman: Mastering the 7 Steps to Personal Power*. Deerfield Beach, FL: Health Communications, Inc.

O'Gorman, P., and P. Diaz. 2013. *Healing Trauma Through Self-Parenting: The Codependency Connection*. Deerfield Beach, FL: Health Communications, Inc.

Oliver-Diaz, P. and P. O'Gorman. 1988. *Twelve Steps to Self-Parenting for Adult Children*. Deerfield Beach, FL: Health Communications, Inc.

Orman, S. 2010. *Women & Money: Owning the Power to Control Your Destiny*. New York: Spiegel & Grau.

Patton, S. 2014. *Marry Smart: Advice for Finding THE ONE*. New York: Gallery Books.

Pauley, J. 2014. *Your Life Calling: Reimagining the Rest of Your Life*. New York: Simon and Schuster.

Perel, E. 2014. "Are We Asking Too Much of Our Spouses?" NPR, April 25. http://www.npr.org/2014/04/25/301825600/are-we-asking-too-much-of-our-spouses

Rankin, L. 2009. "The Doctor Is In: Uncomfortable with Sex." May 28, 2009. http://collegecandy.com/2009/05/28/the-doctor-is-in-uncomfortable-with-sex/

Rezvani, S. 2012. "Mean Girls at Work." *Washington Post*, January 24. http://www.washingtonpost.com/national/on-leadership/mean-girls-at-work/2012/01/24/gIQAu4suNQ_story.html

Roiphe, A. http://thinkexist.com/quotation/a_woman_whose_smile_is_open_and_whose_expression/222481.html. Accessed April 2, 2014.

Samakow, J. 2014. "This Woman Wants to Change How All of Us See Our Bodies." May 14, 2014. http://www.huffingtonpost.com/2014/05/14/embrace-taryn brumfitt_n_5318178.html

Sandberg, S. 2013. *Lean In: Women, Work, and the Will to Lead*. New York: Alfred A. Knopf.

Simmons, R. 2010. *The Curse of the Good Girl: Raising Authentic Girls with Courage and Confidence*. New York: Penguin.

Stark, R. 2014. "Why I Left the Botox Party." *Huffington Post, February 28.* http://www.huffingtonpost.com/rachael-stark/botox-party_b_4802485.html. *2.28.14*

Starr, D. n.d. Student paper. "How Toys Teach Stereotypical Gender Roles: A Look Inside a Local Toy Store." University of North Carolina. http://www.unc.edu/~dcderosa/STUDENTPAPERS/childrenbattles/toysrusdenise.htm

Stockton, C. http://thoughtcatalog.com/christine-stockton/2013/11/61-quotes-that-will-make-you-feel-beautiful-no-matter-how-you-look.

Tan, A. 1989. *The Joy Luck Club.* New York: Penguin.

Tardanico, S. 2011. "Five Tips to Solve the Good Girl Curse." *Forbes,* October 28. http://www.forbes.com/sites/work-in-progress/2011/10/28/five-tips-to-solve-the-good-girl-curse/

Torabi, F. 2014. *When She Makes More: 10 Rules for Breadwinning Women.* New York: Hudson Street Press.

Van Loo, K. J., and R. J. Rydell. 2013. "On the Experience of Feeling Powerful: Perceived Power Moderates the Effect of Stereotype Threat on Women's Math Performance." *Personality and Social Psychology Bulletin* 39(3):387.

Weigel, J. 2013. *This Isn't the Life I Ordered.* Cardiff, Ca: Waterfront Digital Kindle edition.

Wells, T. 2011. *Chasing Youth Culture and Getting It Right: How Your Business Can Profit by Tapping Today's Most Powerful Trendsetters and Tastemakers.* Hoboken, NJ: John Wiley & Sons.

Winerman, L. 2013. "What Draws Us to Facebook?" *APA Monitor* 44(3): page 56.

Wolf, N. 2002. *The Beauty Myth: How Images of Beauty Are Used Against Women.* New York: Harper.

Zakarin, J. "Lake Bell's Nationwide Quest to Stop Women Using 'Sexy Baby Voices.'" Buzzfeed. August 5, 2013. http://www.buzzfeed.com/jordanzakarin/lake-bell-in-a-world-sexy-baby-voice

About the Author

Patricia A. O'Gorman, Ph.D., bestselling author, is an internationally recognized public speaker known for her warm, funny, and inspiring presentations, as well as a resiliency coach and a psychologist. She is noted for her work on women, children of alcoholics, and trauma in the child welfare, mental health, and substance-abuse systems. She has a psychology practice in Saranac Lake, New York.

Dr. O'Gorman serves on the Board of the New York State Coalition Against Sexual Assault, and she previously directed a rape crisis center as well as the Division of Prevention for the National Institute on Alcohol Abuse and Alcoholism. She founded the Department of Prevention and Education for the National Office of the National Council on Alcoholism and Drug Dependence (NCADD), worked as a clinical director and chief psychologist for a statewide child welfare agency, and is a cofounder and current advisory board member of the National Association for Children of Alcoholics. In addition, she is the chairperson of the advisory board of Horses Healing Hearts, Inc. (HHH) a nationally recognized equine therapy program for children of alcoholics located in Delray Beach, Florida.

She is a veteran of numerous radio and television appearances, including *Good Morning America*, *Today*, and *AM Sunday*, and is the author of numerous articles in magazines, including *Addiction Today*, *Counselor*, and *Recovery*, and has been quoted in WebMD.

This is her ninth book, her third in her series on women, which include:

The Resilient Woman:
Mastering the 7 Steps to Personal Power (2013)

Dancing Backwards in High Heels:
How Women Master the Art of Resilience (1994)

Dr. O'Gorman's other books
(coauthored with Phil Diaz, MSW) are:

Healing Trauma Through Self-Parenting:
The Codependency Connection (2013)

The Lowdown on Families Who Get High (2004)

12 Steps to Self-Parenting Workbook (1990)

12 Steps to Self-Parenting for Adult Children (1988)

Breaking the Cycle of Addiction (1987)

and (coauthored with Peter Finn):
Teaching About Alcohol (1980)

Coming soon: *The Man's Guide to Girly Thoughts*

Now that you understand your girly thoughts, help your boyfriend, husband, brother, son, and all the men in your life do the same.

New for 2015! A workbook and curriculum for facilitators working with women: "Out Your Girly Thoughts and Embrace Your Strength," available through *www.patriciaogorman.com*.

Suggested Questions for Book Club Discussions

- How is the concept of girly thoughts helpful in understanding yourself, your original family, and the women around you?

- Has an awareness of girly thoughts helped you become less judgmental of yourself? Of others?

- How has realizing that you are thinking girly thoughts helped you in your primary intimate relationship? Do you find you are freer to be yourself here? Are you arguing less? Enjoying yourself more? Feeling more sexy?

- How does the concept of girly thoughts help you appreciate how you have been "misdirected" by the media? Do you find yourself focused on your clothing, weight, and appearance instead of putting your energy into mastering your personal goals of education, work success, having a successful intimate relationship, or parenting?

- Thinking about advertising you've seen, name some ads that make you angry because they exploit women's fears. What action would you like to take?

- How is it helpful to understand that your mother had girly thoughts?

- What do you find helpful in Dr. O'Gorman not only giving you a list of girly thoughts but also explaining where each one comes from and what you can do to challenge these specific thoughts?

- What girly thoughts do you find most prevalent at work? In managing your finances? When you are in public situations? Among your friends? In your marriage, or dating? With your children?

- Does having the concept of girly thoughts make it possible to stop taking things so personally, particularly at work, at home, with your friends, and with your original family members?

- What was your reaction to realizing that your girly thoughts have stopped you from feeling beautiful?

- In which area of your life has reading this book made the most impact?

- Why would you recommend *The Girly Thoughts 10-Day Detox Plan* to someone?